The Beginner's Guide to
Receiving the Holy Spirit

The Beginner's Guide to Receiving the Holy Spirit

QUIN SHERRER
and
RUTHANNE GARLOCK

VINE BOOKS

SERVANT PUBLICATIONS
ANN ARBOR, MICHIGAN

Vine Books is an imprint of Servant Publications especially designed to serve evangelical Christians.

Servant Publications—Mission Statement
We are dedicated to publishing books that spread the gospel of Jesus Christ, help Christians to live in accordance with that gospel, promote renewal in the church, and bear witness to Christian unity.

The personal stories that appear in this book are true, but names of some individuals have been changed to protect their privacy.

Published by Servant Publications
P.O. Box 8617
Ann Arbor, Michigan 48107
www.servantpub.com

Cover design: Alan Furst, Inc., Minneapolis, Minn.

02 03 04 05 10 9 8 7 6 5 4 3 2 1

Printed in the United States of America
ISBN 1-56955-275-4

Library of Congress Cataloging-in-Publication Data

Sherrer, Quin.
　　The beginner's guide to receiving the Holy Spirit / Quin Sherrer and Ruthanne Garlock.
　　　　p. cm.
　　Includes bibliographical references.
　　ISBN 1-56955-275-4 (alk. paper)
　　1. Holy Spirit. 2. Baptism in the Holy Spirit. 3. Gifts, Spiritual.
　　4. Fruit of the Spirit. 5. Pentecostalism. I. Garlock, Ruthanne. II.
　　Title.
　　BT123 .S46 2002
　　234'.13--dc21
　　　　　　　　　　　　　　　　　　　　　　　　　　　　　　200200153

Contents

Acknowledgments

I (Quin) thank the Lord Jesus for sending the Holy Spirit to dwell in his believers after he returned to heaven.

I will be forever grateful to the Reverend Forrest Mobley, an Episcopal priest in Destin, Florida, who lovingly encouraged me to receive the baptism of the Holy Spirit back in the early 1970s. In obedience to the Lord, Forrest had allowed the late Reverend Dennis Bennett to pray for him and his wife Nancy to receive the Holy Spirit three years earlier—a "risky" action for mainline ministers in those days.

I am also grateful for John Sherrill, whose book, *They Speak with Other Tongues*, helped me understand the gift of the Holy Spirit, and for John and Elizabeth's role in my writing career as I studied under them the year following my encounter with the Holy Spirit.

I (Ruthanne) acknowledge the late Reverends John and Lydia Stubblefield, my pastors during my growing-up years in Tulsa, Oklahoma, who mentored me in the ways of the Holy Spirit. Their example gave me a determination to serve the Lord with my whole heart and to never turn back.

I also express appreciation for Jeri Livingston, the now-retired evangelist's wife who prayed with me the night I received the Holy Spirit, more than fifty years ago.

Both of us are grateful for our special friends at Servant—Don Cooper, Bert Ghezzi, Dorothy Griffin, and Kathy Deering—who have helped and encouraged us over the past dozen years that we've been writing for Vine Books. Their vision and commitment to Christian publishing has brought enlightenment and blessing to multitudes.

Thanks also to the men and women who were willing to share their stories with you, our readers, in the hope that your lives may also be touched by the Holy Spirit.

Introduction

I was thrilled to be attending this wedding of Nan and Joe in a stone chapel overlooking the breathtaking snowcapped Colorado mountains near Vail. The ceremony was an answer to the prayers our family had prayed for Nan, now in her late thirties, who had waited many years for a Christian husband.

As they exchanged vows, my thoughts drifted back to a night eight years earlier when Nan had been a guest in our home. She and our daughter had moved from Dallas to Colorado to be roommates and were staying with us as they hunted for jobs and a house to rent.

One Wednesday night Nan went with us to a service at our small interdenominational church. Since she'd been raised in a strict denominational setting, our style of worship seemed a bit strange to her. Our pastor taught about receiving the baptism of the Holy Spirit. Later, as we sat around our dining table that night, snacking, she plied us with questions:

Wasn't I filled with the Holy Spirit when I accepted Christ as a child?

Why do I need another experience?

What will the Holy Spirit do for me—will I know God better?

Do I have to speak in tongues?

On and on the questions went. I answered as best I could, while encouraging her to continue the seeking process she had begun. Nan began attending our church regularly, no longer considering our services "strange." Many times I saw her face light up with the joy of the Lord as we sang praises to him. I don't know whether she ever prayed to receive the Holy Spirit, but she did become comfortable worshipping with Spirit-filled people. At her wedding, at the request of the bride and groom, the minister invited anyone present who did not know Jesus personally to accept him right then and there.

In the years that followed, as I tried to explain to many other Nans the benefits of receiving the baptism of the Holy Spirit, I dreamed of writing a book for beginners on this topic. I even wrote out a two-page handout to give to those who asked me similar questions.

When our friends at Servant asked Ruthanne and me to write *The Beginner's Guide to Receiving the Holy Spirit,* we jumped at the opportunity. I remembered my own experience, many years ago, when I'd had a multitude of doubts and questions, just like Nan's.

We were in the middle of writing this book when, on September 11, 2001, terrorist suicide pilots destroyed the World Trade Center in New York and struck the U.S. Pentagon. The horror of the attack and the huge loss of life left Americans numb with shock. In the following days and weeks our nation turned to God, led by our president. The Holy Spirit was present, even in the midst of the tragedy, ministering to people in all walks of life. We heard many stories of God's protection, direction, and comfort, both during the crisis and beyond.

For instance, AnneMarie, my friend who lives in New York, had spent twenty years trying to get her neighbor to accept the Lord. She showered her with kindness, holiday gifts, and backyard fence talks. On the night of September 11, with AnneMarie present, this neighbor not only accepted the Lord, she received the baptism of the Holy Spirit—all in the same evening!

Just a few weeks after the attack, I was scheduled to teach a seminar on prayer at a large church on the West Coast. "Before

September 11, I wouldn't have said that we were a praying church," the leader told me plainly. "But now we're open for the Holy Spirit to teach us how to pray." On a Friday night—an evening when church members usually attended sports events—the place was packed as people came for a two-hour session on how to pray.

Afterward, a pastor's wife from another church asked me to pray for her to receive the baptism of the Holy Spirit, though she said her husband and church would not approve. "I'm so hungry for more of the Lord—for the Holy Spirit to minister to me, so I will be better equipped to minister to our congregation," she said.

Two months after giving me her story for this book (chapter 3), my friend Hilda lost her husband to heart disease. She is feeling the Holy Spirit's comfort today, just as she felt his joy and love the night she knelt in her den more than thirty years ago to welcome the Holy Spirit into her life.

In these pages you will meet many people who have received this gift and discovered the empowerment, guidance, and comfort of the Holy Spirit in their everyday lives. It is our hope that you, as a seeker, will find here the biblical answers to your questions, and that you will receive the precious gift the Lord has for you.

We pray you will develop an intimate relationship with the Third Person of the Trinity, so that as you arise each morning you can say, "Holy Spirit, you are welcome in my life today. Speak to me. Love through me. Come, direct my every step, my every conversation, my every decision."

You will discover that no matter what the future holds, you can rely upon the Holy Spirit to sustain and guide you in every situation.

—*Quin Sherrer*

ONE

Who Is the Holy Spirit?

You will receive power when the Holy Spirit comes on you; and you will be my witnesses in Jerusalem, and in all Judea and Samaria, and to the ends of the earth.... All of them were filled with the Holy Spirit and began to speak in other tongues as the Spirit enabled them.

ACTS 1:8; 2:4

Power? Holy Spirit? Tongues? Does this all sound "far out" to you?

Many people shy away from these topics because they feel they're too controversial, or because they think they're too hard to understand. Some tend to think of the Holy Spirit as a ghostly, ethereal entity not related to real life in today's world. Yet the exact opposite is true.

Jesus told his followers that he would not always be physically present with them, but he would ask the Father to send "another Helper, that He may abide with you forever" (Jn 14:16, NKJV). That Helper is the Holy Spirit—the Third Person of the Trinity. The Triune God consists of three Persons or entities—Father, Son, and Holy Spirit. Theologian J.I. Packer explains that the three "are always together and always cooperating, with the Father initiating, the Son complying, and the Spirit executing the will of both, which is his will also."[1]

When we examine the Scriptures, we find that God has much to teach us about the Holy Spirit. In this book we will explore the significance of the Holy Spirit and learn about the wonderful gift that is available to every believer. The following story is an example of a seeker who pursued such a quest for truth.

Thirsty for More

"What is the Holy Spirit?"

That was Katy's question to the woman with whom she'd been chatting as they waited in the food line at a church picnic, when Rena mentioned that the Lord had been speaking to her about the Holy Spirit.

Noting Katy's interest, Rena went on to share how she had been baptized in the Holy Spirit, had spoken in tongues, and was hungry to learn more about this gift.

"I knew the 'Holy Ghost' was included in the Apostles' Creed, which I recited every Sunday, and was mentioned at baptisms and in benediction prayers," Katy reported. "But I'd never heard a Bible lesson or sermon about the Holy Spirit. My relationship with Christ was genuine, but I was thirsty for more. I had just received my officer's commission in the Army as a nurse and was at a hinge-point in my life."

For five weeks Katy sought in every way possible to learn more about the Holy Spirit. One night at a meeting of the Officers' Christian Fellowship she was full of questions.

"Would you like to receive the Holy Spirit?" the Bible teacher asked after answering several queries.

"Yes!" Katy responded eagerly, following the Bible teacher and her husband to a back room for prayer.

They laid hands on her and prayed, then led Katy in a prayer asking the Holy Spirit to fill her to overflowing. Suddenly she felt an overwhelming sense of God's love and peace. The experience so changed Katy's demeanor that her colleagues noticed the difference the very next day.

A Stream of Strength

"I was so thrilled with this marvelous peace, I decided it wasn't really necessary for me to speak in tongues," Katy said. "But the couple who had prayed for me to receive the Holy Spirit gently encouraged me to remain open to the idea. They taught me a lot about the gifts of the Holy Spirit and the many ways he works in our lives by showing me both the power and the fruit of the Holy Spirit."

Six months later, at a Christmas party, another friend prayed for Katy to receive her prayer language, and she haltingly spoke a few words. "A fluency in tongues didn't come right away, because of my resistance," she admitted. "But later, when I began struggling with problems in my marriage, I began praying in tongues in my private prayer time. Gradually it began to flow more easily. Rather than a 'gusher' experience such as some of my friends had told about, it seemed the Holy Spirit was 'drip-feeding' me with a steady stream of strength and courage on a day-to-day basis."

Katy discovered that receiving this gift was not merely a one-time event—though her first encounter with the Holy Spirit was a spiritual milestone she will always remember. Rather, she's learned that the Holy Spirit living within her enables her to tap into his strength, wisdom, and power as she encounters life's challenges. Today, many years later, Katy prays in tongues for all kinds of situations, but mostly when she is praying alone.

God's Gift for All His Children

After his resurrection and just before he ascended to heaven, Jesus appeared to his followers and promised that his Father would send them the Holy Spirit. He instructed them to wait in Jerusalem for this to happen, telling them that when the Holy Spirit came they would be "clothed with power."

This word *power*—derived from the Greek word *dunamis*, from which we get the words *dynamo* or *dynamite*—also means ability, strength, or a person who has administrative power.[2] In other words, Jesus was telling them that the Holy Spirit would empower and equip them to fulfill their assignment to carry the gospel message to the ends of the earth (see Mt 28:19-20; Acts 1:8).

Women, including Mary, the mother of Jesus, were present when the 120 believers experienced the outpouring of the Holy Spirit in the Upper Room (see Acts 1:14). Obviously, Jesus intended this gift for *all* believers, not just the twelve apostles. All of them heard a rushing, mighty wind, saw fire descend from heaven, and began speaking in languages they had never learned (see Acts 2:1-4).

The apostle Peter explained the phenomenon to the astonished crowd that gathered, then declared: "The promise is for you and your children and for all who are far off—for all whom the Lord our God will call" (Acts 2:39).

Historians generally agree that this event marks the beginning of the church age. Yet many also have taught that miraculous signs recorded in Scripture, such as speaking in tongues or healing, were only for the early church—not for believers today. This view, called *cessationism*, holds that such signs are no longer necessary because we now have the written Word of God.

Sadly, this teaching, which dictates restrictions on the work of the Holy Spirit, has caused thousands of believers to miss the blessings the Holy Spirit wants to pour into their lives. In fact, this mind-set is the reason many believers, such as Katy, have grown up in churches where the Holy Spirit was rarely mentioned at all.

Yet, history records countless instances of hungry seekers asking for the gift Jesus promised and receiving the Holy Spirit, often with the outward sign of speaking in tongues. These believers feel they're included in the "all who are far off" group mentioned in Peter's sermon (Acts 2:39), and they have embraced the blessing.

Reborn by the Spirit

If you have truly been born again, it was the Holy Spirit who convicted you of sin, revealed to you the truth of the gospel, and drew you into relationship with Christ. The following verses emphasize this truth:

> For you did not receive a spirit that makes you a slave again to fear, but you received the Spirit of sonship. And by him we cry, "Abba, Father." The Spirit himself testifies with our spirit that we are God's children.
>
> ROMANS 8:15-16

> No one who is speaking by the Spirit of God says, "Jesus be cursed," and no one can say, "Jesus is Lord," except by the Holy Spirit.
>
> 1 CORINTHIANS 12:3

The Holy Spirit definitely is with you from the time of your conversion. Yet the baptism of the Holy Spirit we're speaking of here, and which Katy received, is subsequent to the salvation experience, as Pastor Jack Hayford explains:

> The Holy Spirit's power must be "received"; it is not an automatic experience. As surely as the Holy Spirit indwells each believer (Romans 8:9), so surely will He fill and overflow each who receives the Holy Spirit in childlike faith (John 7:37-39). When the Holy Spirit fills you, you will know it. Jesus said it and the disciples found it true (Acts 1:4; 2:1-4).[3]

A Divine Appointment

Sometimes, as in Debbie's case, you can receive the gift of salvation and the baptism of the Holy Spirit at the same time.

Debbie had been reared in a cult-type religion. All she knew about Jesus was that he was "a good man," someone after whom she could pattern her life. One day she attended a Christian meeting with a friend. After the lively music and preaching—which did not offend her or turn her off—she heard a still, small voice speak to her. She recognized it as a holy voice.

"Debbie, I want you."

"Yes, Lord, I want you, too," she responded.

"I want you to walk closer to me."

"Yes, Lord, I want to walk closer to you," she said.

At the end of the meeting, when the speaker invited those who wanted prayer to come to the front of the auditorium, Debbie practically ran to get there.

"What do you want?" the prayer counselor asked her.

"I want to walk closer to the Lord."

The counselor encouraged her to confess her sins and ask Jesus to be her personal Lord. Debbie did that, then she heard herself say, "Lord, I love you. . . . Lord, I love you." She had truly been born again.

Next, she began to speak in a language she had never learned. She was puzzled until the counselor explained that she was experiencing the baptism of the Holy Spirit, which she could later read about in the Book of Acts. Joy overflowed from her, and she continued speaking in tongues even after she returned to her seat. That was twenty years ago.

Debbie has since been to many nations, teaching the Scripture and praying for dozens to receive the baptism of the Holy Spirit. Her husband, who was at first skeptical about this gift, received the baptism in the Holy Spirit in a dramatic encounter while on a tour in Israel. Since then he has accompanied his wife on several overseas mission trips.

Debbie acknowledges that she was spiritually hungry—otherwise she wouldn't even have agreed to attend the meeting with her friend. Yet God had an appointment with her, and he used her friend to see that she didn't miss it.[4]

A Simple Prayer Changed Her Life

Leslyn's story reveals the power of the Holy Spirit to transform a person's life through physical healing. Her spiritual journey began with a radical conversion experience when she was only fourteen years old. Yet, certain areas of sin from her past kept cropping up, and she was repeatedly asking God for forgiveness. Four years later, she reached a turning point during her first year of college, when she suddenly passed out in the school library. She tells her story:

As I came to, I realized that numbness was moving through the entire left side of my body—the beginning of a progressive paralysis that seemed to grow worse every day. Eventually I had to take medical leave from college and move back home to undergo a myriad of tests. All the doctors could tell me was that the paralysis appeared to be permanent and was getting worse. They did not know what caused it.

I knew Jesus and had committed my life to him as a young teenager. But it was embarrassing to come to him over and over, asking forgiveness for the same things. I simply didn't have the strength to overcome the sinful behavior in my life.

Shortly before starting college, I had gone on a mission trip and met a woman who seemed to have a power in her life that I had never encountered before. I was skeptical and even a little afraid of someone like her. She talked about speaking in tongues, which I had been taught was from the devil. I kept my distance and never allowed her to pray for me, yet I couldn't stop thinking about the power and joy in her life.

Now, facing permanent paralysis at age eighteen, I knew I desperately needed more of God in my life. I was sick of sin, afraid of the future, and I wanted to somehow walk through this illness closer to the Lord. I had read in the Book of Acts that the disciples received power to become God's witnesses when the Holy Spirit came on them. The woman I had met on the mission trip said the power in her life came from the Holy Spirit. If ever in my life I needed what she had, it was now.

One day while lying in bed I simply prayed, "God, I desperately need your help. I need your power to be able to face the future and to gain victory over the sin in my life that seems to prevail. Lord, I need more of you—come and fill me with your Holy Spirit."

The Lord was just waiting for me to ask! Suddenly, a warmth spread through my body and I felt as light as a feather. Fear of the future melted away because I was certain that the Lord would be there with me to face whatever might come. Faith displaced my fears and I fell asleep thanking him for filling me. I had no idea how dramatically that simple prayer would change my life. Though I did not speak in tongues at that time, God was gracious in giving me other gifts that I would soon begin to discover.

A few hours later I awoke with an awareness that God was asking me to pray for a friend. I had never experienced such a strong urgency to pray for someone before, nor had the Lord ever awakened me in the middle of the night. As I prayed, the Holy Spirit spoke very specific things to me to pray for that person—things I did not know in the natural. This was all very new to me, but I prayed the things the Lord had put on my heart and then went back to sleep.

The next night the same thing happened. A week later the Lord asked me to write a letter to this person and tell her about the things he had told me to pray for her. It was one thing to pray for her in private, but actually telling her was another! After arguing with God for a couple of days, I wrote the letter. My friend wrote back that what I had shared was exactly what she was going through, and she knew that only God could have told me those things. Now I was a little "freaked out," because I didn't understand what was going on in my life. But God provided an answer.

Though weak and still partially paralyzed, I made a trip back to my college town to visit friends. While there I confided in a dear friend and her roommate about the unusual experiences I was having. My friend's roommate explained from the Scripture about the gifts of prophecy and words of knowledge. At the time I'd received Christ I had renounced all occultic practices and influences in my life and determined to have nothing to do with anything supernatural. I had been taught that supernatural occurrences in the Bible passed away with the original apostles—a teaching I liked because it felt safe and suited my analytical mind.

But at last I was beginning to realize that God is the same yesterday, today, and forever. The Holy Spirit is still alive and well ... still empowering his people ... still giving gifts to his church. God had answered my prayer to be filled with the Spirit beyond all that I could have asked for or imagined, and that was only the beginning.

The Holy Spirit Brings Healing

About a month later, God began a miraculous healing in my partially paralyzed body. After two days of feeling progressively stronger, I woke up on the third day completely healed. I had no weakness, and the atrophy that had begun in my muscles was gone. It truly was a miracle. Doctors had no explanation.

At that point, as I returned to everyday life, I realized just how significantly the Holy Spirit had changed me. Realizing it was time to rethink my stance on the gifts of the Holy Spirit, I began talking with friends to get their insight, only to learn that God also was changing their preconceived ideas about the Holy Spirit. We began meeting between classes at the local junior college we were attending, to discover the truth about the gifts of the Spirit.

Then I went with one of these friends to a home meeting of a charismatic prayer group and heard people speak and sing in tongues for the first time. The harmonies were unlike anything I had ever heard, and the intensity and duration of the singing seemed to ebb and flow in unison like a choir directed by the Holy Spirit. Afterward, I spoke for more than an hour with the woman in whose home the group met. She patiently explained the Scriptures to me and answered my seemingly endless questions about the Holy Spirit and speaking in tongues.

I got home about midnight, went directly to my room, and reread all the verses she had shared with me that night. The Scripture was clear—tongues was a legitimate gift of the Holy Spirit for believers today. One verse seemed to jump off the page: "Therefore, brethren, desire earnestly to prophesy, and do not forbid to speak with tongues" (1 Cor 14:39, NKJV).

I took out a legal pad and made two columns, listing the "pros" and "cons" of speaking in tongues. On the "con" side, I had a long list of people's opinions that I had heard over the years as to why one should not speak in tongues. On the "pro" side, I wrote the single sentence I had read in the Bible that said to not forbid speaking in tongues. Then I prayed a simple prayer: "Lord, if you want me to have this gift, I want it."

Immediately I began to hear words in my mind—such as when you "hear" yourself thinking. But I didn't recognize any of the words. In faith, I began to speak out the words that I was hearing in my mind. It felt awkward, as anything does for the first time, but I continued praying in this new language for about forty-five minutes. Then I went to bed.

I had been baptized in the Holy Spirit five months before, but God had gently and patiently brought me to a place where I could receive all that he had for me. The gift of tongues revolutionized my worship and prayer life. I found that I could express the deep things of my heart to the Lord, whereas before I could only say, "Lord, I don't know how to pray about this— I have no words to express what I am feeling or thinking."

With the gift of tongues my prayer and praise were no longer limited by my native language; my spirit was unfettered. I found that as I prayed in tongues about difficult situations, understanding and wisdom would begin to come which enabled me to pray more accurately in English.

I also found that the negative things people had told me about tongues were not true at all. For instance, I was told that speaking in tongues could not be controlled. That scared me. I was also mistakenly told that if the gift of tongues was really from God, the words would just start coming out of my mouth without me initiating it on my own. But I discovered that speaking in tongues is very much like singing. I can choose to sing or I can choose not to sing. I don't just start singing uncontrollably, nor does it suddenly just "come over me." Rather, I hear a melody in my mind or want to express my heart through song and so I begin to sing. It is the same with the gift of tongues. It is given by the Holy Spirit, but it is up to my discretion to receive and exercise that gift.

My life changed radically after that five-month encounter with the Holy Spirit. Within two years I was living in Asia, where I served as a missionary with Youth With A Mission (YWAM) for six years. I met and married my husband during that time, and we have been blessed with two children who love the Lord. For more than twenty years, God's grace and the transforming power of the Holy Spirit have enabled me to serve him. I am hungrier for more of God's Spirit today than I have ever been. I eagerly look forward to continuing to learn how to better partner with the Spirit's work in the lives of others. I want to continually walk in more of God's power to see lives changed and transformed into the image of Jesus.

Why Did God Choose Tongues?

The phenomenon of speaking in tongues is a major stumbling block for many who say, "I want the Holy Spirit, but I don't want to speak in tongues. Why did God choose tongues, anyway?" J. Rodman Williams offers this insight:

From the Pentecostal narrative [Acts 2:7-11 and 10:44-47] it is apparent that tongues are not ordinary speech, but represent the worship of God in a speech that is other than one's own native language. Hence, speaking in tongues might be called *transcendent praise:* praise that goes beyond ordinary capacity and experience.

... Ordinary language, even music, may be inadequate to declare the wonder of God's gift.... There may be a speech or language more suitable to the experience of the richness of God's spiritual gift. Humanly speaking, this is impossible, but God through his Spirit may go beyond what has been uttered or sung before and bring forth a new language![5]

Our human minds cannot comprehend all God's purposes, for he is sovereign. Yet Scripture does tell us why God confused the languages in the first place. Evil men—envisioning an empire where they would have total control—began building the Tower of Babel. This was God's response:

The Lord said, "If as one people speaking the same language they have begun to do this, then nothing they plan to do will be impossible for them. Come, let us go down and confuse their language so they will not understand each other." So the Lord scattered them from there over all the earth, and they stopped building the city. That is why it was called Babel—because there the Lord confused the language of the whole world. From there the Lord scattered them over the face of the whole earth.

GENESIS 11:6-9

A noted nineteenth-century Bible teacher writes that in Genesis 11, God confused the languages as an expression of his *judgment*, while in Acts 2 he gave various tongues as an expression of his *grace*. Yet in Revelation 7, "we see all those tongues gathered round the Lamb in *glory*."[6]

I (Ruthanne) once heard Bible teacher Roberta Hromas, granddaughter of Pentecostal pioneer Charles F. Parham, say this: "When God took his finger of fire and set it upon each one of those in the Upper Room, he wrote a new law of love in their hearts and gave them a new language that superseded the languages he had given at the Tower of Babel. Those languages brought confusion and competition. But as we receive this new language of the law of love within us, we need not walk in the confusion or competition of Babel."

What About Emotionalism?

Some argue against contemporary manifestations of the Holy Spirit, claiming that people too often get caught up in emotional excesses. Of course abuses occur from time to time. People who receive the Holy Spirit don't become instantly perfect. They are vulnerable to making the mistake of placing too much emphasis on one particular gift, falling into error or spiritual pride, or simply exhibiting immaturity and poor judgment. Yet, occasional abuses do not warrant discrediting the

Holy Spirit's work in the lives of believers today.

I (Quin) remember a formal Christmas dinner party held by my husband's office back in the early 1970s, before we had received the Holy Spirit. The wife of one of my husband's colleagues introduced herself to guests by saying, "Hi, I'm Beth [not her real name], and I have been baptized in the Holy Spirit. Can I share with you how it will change your life?" People, including me, squirmed and made excuses to get away from her. It seemed that everything she said was punctuated by such expressions as, "Well, praise the Lord. Oh, thank you, Jesus."

As one who had not yet had this experience, I even questioned her sanity. How much more appropriate it would have been, had she allowed God to lead her to speak privately to someone whose heart was prepared and open. A year later I was ready to hear what she had to say. Thankfully, by then she had matured and was able to explain her life-changing experience in a way I could comprehend. So, if you have been exposed to some of these excesses, don't let it deter you from embracing the blessing of being baptized in the Holy Spirit. I'm very glad I didn't let that uncomfortable encounter with Beth keep me from receiving this gift.

Later in the book we'll deal with some pitfalls to avoid. First, however, we encourage you to get acquainted with the Holy Spirit as a person who wants to dwell within you and continually guide you. In the next chapter you will discover some of the ways the Holy Spirit can make a difference in your life.

Prayer

Thank you, Lord, for helping me to understand more clearly the importance of the Holy Spirit in my life. I want to be open to learning more and more about this gift you have given. Help me to apply the truth of your Word as the Holy Spirit reveals it to me. Amen.

TWO

Does the Holy Spirit Make a Difference?

When [Peter and John] arrived, they prayed for [the Samaritans] that they might receive the Holy Spirit, because the Holy Spirit had not yet come upon any of them; they had simply been baptized into the name of the Lord Jesus. Then Peter and John placed their hands on them, and they received the Holy Spirit.

ACTS 8:15-17

By inviting the Holy Spirit to work more deeply in our lives, we who long for more of God can discover a deeper level of intimacy with him. That's what I (Quin) experienced one night in a little church in Destin, Florida. I was amazed to learn that the Holy Spirit desires to completely indwell every believer.

Revealing New Truth

The worship service was so foreign to me. Men and women were raising their hands in praise to God and singing from the Bible. To me, it was mind-boggling. I frowned and gave Mom a questioning look. "Those are Scripture choruses," she whispered, smiling and joining in.

I was visiting St. Andrews Episcopal Church with Mom simply because she insisted it was a good way to spend a Thursday night. Besides, she wanted me to meet some of her new friends, since she'd recently retired here.

Mom had reared us in a liturgical church, though it wasn't Episcopal, and I don't remember a time when I didn't love Jesus and pray to the Father. Yet the Holy Spirit was barely mentioned, except in formal prayers and the singing of the doxology. I was accustomed to a fixed form of worship: an opening prayer, the singing of three traditional hymns, the passing of the offering plates, listening to a twenty-minute sermon, and leaving after the benediction. One hour on Sunday morning and we were ready for lunch.

Now I was in my thirties, with three children, and my husband and I were rearing them in the same tradition. Yet here, in this crowded little church with people standing in the aisles, I encountered the *presence* of the Holy Spirit for the first time.

I watched in amazement as a grown man, with hands upraised, began softly praising the Lord with tears rolling down his cheeks. "Jesus, I love you. Jesus, I praise you. Jesus, I thank you for providing a way to heaven for me," he whispered. The sights and sounds captivated me. Though the service lasted more than two hours, it seemed like only moments. In my heart I knew that these people knew Jesus at a depth that I didn't. I yearned to have what they had.

As I left the meeting I swallowed my pride and asked the pastor, Forrest Mobley, "What makes these people so different from me and other Christians I know? I've taught Sunday school most of my life, and Jesus is my Savior, but I don't worship like these folks. How can I do it?"

"Most of these who come to worship on Thursday night have received the baptism in the Holy Spirit—the gift Jesus told his followers he would send before he went back to heaven," Pastor Mobley told me.

"You mean I can receive it, too?" I asked.

"Of course you can," he responded. "After our Thursday

meetings, those who are interested in more instruction can come to my office. First I teach, then I pray for them to be filled with power—or, as Jesus called it, 'baptized with the Holy Spirit.'"

"I'll have to give this more thought," I said, shaking his hand. I was wondering silently, *Is this Holy Spirit the same as the Holy Ghost we sing about in the doxology?*

"Well, if you're serious," the pastor interrupted my thoughts, "reread the first four chapters of Acts, then come ask me some more questions. But read with an open mind, asking God to reveal the truth to you."

Since I'd be visiting Mom another ten days, I promised to do that.

Healing Prayer

The next night I attended a home prayer meeting where a group from St. Andrews had gathered. As about a dozen of us sat or knelt in prayer, the shrill ring of the telephone distracted my attention. Betty, our hostess, slipped out to answer the phone in the hall while everyone else kept on praying. Everyone, that is, except me. Being unaccustomed to praying aloud, I just sat there listening.

Some were praying softly in languages I'd never heard before. Others were thanking God for healing some man named Bill. These people talked to God as if they knew him intimately! I envied that, yet it bewildered me. Betty returned and softly announced, "That was a message about Bill Lance. The doctors at the Air Force hospital in Mississippi say he is dying tonight. Let's pray in agreement right now for his life to be spared."

Then Betty prayed aloud while the others listened: "Lord, we've already had a healing service for Bill at our church. Now we believe you are restoring him, regardless of what the doctors say. So we stand in agreement and thank you in advance for his healing."

Someone in the room spoke aloud. "Satan, we give notice that you and your demonic forces cannot have Bill Lance. He is God's property, and we are standing in the gap for his complete healing. Spirits of infirmity, leave him, in Jesus' name."

Betty leaned toward me and quietly explained that Bill Lance was a new Christian, a thirty-one-year-old Air Force captain stationed at a nearby base. "He and his wife Sharon have two young children," she said. "The doctors say he's dying with acute leukemia. Tonight he's in critical condition, so prayer groups all over town are being called. Yet we've had the assurance God is going to heal Bill. He's got the assurance, too, so we'll keep on praying."

I bowed my head. "Lord, listen to Betty's prayers—to all their prayers—just count mine out. I don't know whether you still heal today, but I'm willing to learn, Lord. Show me."

I was really puzzled. Was God still in the healing business? I'd been taught in my church that healing went out with the apostles, along with that part in the New Testament about speaking in tongues. Yet, tonight, I sensed something dynamic in the way these people prayed.

Before the meeting ended, I was sure I wanted to know Jesus as personally as they did. Furthermore, I wanted to pray and praise God in my own prayer language.

A Night Never to Forget

I knew Jesus was my Savior, but now I had to admit I had not allowed him to be Lord of my life. The following Thursday night I was back at St. Andrews, and after the meeting I joined a handful of others in the pastor's study for more instruction.

"Although his eleven closest disciples had been with Jesus almost constantly for some three years, he still told them and the other followers to 'stay in the city until you have been clothed with power from on high' (Lk 24:49)," the pastor said. "Why? Because they were going to need the power of the Holy Spirit, once Jesus ascended back to heaven. Tonight we are going to pray together, confess our sins, and ask the Holy Spirit to be in charge of our lives. Then you will receive a new prayer language. Praying in tongues bypasses our minds, enabling our spirits to speak directly to God through the Holy Spirit."

What followed the Bible lesson that night in Pastor Mobley's office thirty years ago totally changed my life. He asked each of us to put into our own words a prayer patterned after this one:

Jesus, I acknowledge you as my Lord and Savior. I ask you to forgive my sins: the wrong things I've done, and things I've failed to do—the things I remember and those I don't. I choose to forgive all who have hurt or wounded me; I free them from any bondage I've held them in through my unforgiveness. If I have ever made fun of anyone who spoke in tongues, please forgive me. Lord, I receive your forgiveness for my sins.

I renounce any involvement with the occult—whether I participated in it knowingly or unknowingly—including reading horoscopes, attending seances, playing occult games, mind reading, fortune-telling, or anything related to the kingdom of darkness. I renounce the devil and all his works. Lord, I now ask to receive the baptism in the Holy Spirit and to speak in a new tongue. In the name of Jesus Christ, I receive in faith. Amen.

Pastor Mobley laid hands on each of us and prayed that the spiritual gifts from 1 Corinthians 12:8-10 would be imparted to us as he called them out: word of wisdom, word of knowledge, faith, healing, working of miracles, prophecy, discerning of spirits, various kinds of tongues, interpretation of tongues. Then he asked God to give us the fruit of the Spirit as mentioned in Galatians 5.

I timidly spoke only three little unfamiliar syllables. They sounded so elementary to me. Was this really praying in tongues, or did I make it up? How glad I was for the warning Pastor Mobley gave after the meeting.

"Don't let the devil tell you you did not speak in tongues tonight," he cautioned. "God gave you that gift of the Holy Spirit. And just as a baby learns to talk with only a few sounds at first, so your prayer language begins with a few syllables, then will expand, increase, and often change."

It was a night I was never to forget. An overpowering love for God and people began to engulf me—especially love and forgiveness for my dad, who had abandoned our family when I was twelve years old.

Renewal Hits Home

When I left Mom's place to return home a few days later, I was definitely changed. I laughed more. I studied the Bible with a new hunger. I even started praying for some close friends to be healed. Amazingly, some were instantly healed!

The Holy Spirit was so real to me, the words of familiar church hymns now held new meaning. I had a new appreciation for the first question from the Westminster Catechism:

Q: What is the chief end of man?
A: Man's chief end is to glorify God and enjoy him forever.

I'd memorized this as a child, but now I was learning what it meant to glorify God, and I was enjoying his presence in my life. My husband, LeRoy, who was an elder in our church, watched me for six months. Finally one day he walked up behind me and put his arms around me while I was in the kitchen. "Whatever happened to you when you visited your mom last summer, I need it too," he said. "You've changed so much, and I want to have the same experience."

"It's called the baptism of the Holy Spirit," I smiled. "But I honestly don't know how to help you receive it—I'm too new myself. Let's call a pastor I've heard about and ask him to pray with you."

After special prayer, LeRoy received the Holy Spirit and spoke in tongues. Then he began loving and encouraging others as he'd never done before. Now, when I wanted to go hear a Christian speaker—even a hundred miles away—he would drive me. We didn't go alone. We loaded up our station wagon with our children and friends who expressed a spiritual hunger. Before long we were hosting two Bible studies a week in our home.

Miracle Story

The following summer, when I returned to Destin to visit Mom, I stopped at the church office the first afternoon to see Pastor Mobley.

"Quin, come back here and meet Bill Lance; I think you should write his testimony, since he's our church's first healing miracle," he exclaimed when he saw me. "Remember how we were all praying for Bill to be healed from leukemia last summer?"

I followed him into the church library, half expecting to meet an emaciated man with thinning hair. Instead, the man, dressed in jeans and a sport shirt, who thrust his hand out to shake mine was robust and exuberant. His round face glowed with health and happiness, and he had a thick mane of hair. A short time later, I wrote his healing testimony, and the story won the prestigious *Guideposts Magazine* Writer's Contest, enabling me to learn from the best of Christian writers at *Guideposts* in New York.

I'm happy to report that, all these years later, Bill Lance is still very much alive and well. He's established his own business and now lives in Colorado, not far from us. Furthermore, Pastor Mobley is still praying for folks to receive the baptism of the Holy Spirit.

I'm no longer hesitant to introduce people to Jesus, or to pray for their healing. My prayer language has definitely become fluent since those first halting syllables. In fact, I've prayed for scores of people to receive this gift.

Power to Witness

Jesus declared that after receiving the Holy Spirit, his followers would have power to be his witnesses (see Acts 1:8). I found that now I had the boldness to share the Lord and pray with people—something that I had never done before. I talked to schoolteachers, the principal, my mailman, my butcher, people in the supermarket. I even asked my newspaper editor to allow me to write a "Fortress of Faith" page each Friday to include Christian testimonies of community leaders and feature articles on local pastors and their churches. This gave me opportunity to meet almost every pastor in town, and all I wanted to talk about was Jesus and my newfound love for him.

My best friend, Lib, who with her husband had gone with us to several full gospel meetings, watched me with great curiosity for several months. Finally she admitted that she, too, yearned for the baptism of the Holy Spirit. "But I'm just not good enough, Quin—I can't ask Jesus for this gift," she kept telling me. I couldn't convince her the gift was for her.

One day she said it again, crying buckets of tears. "No, Lib, you aren't good enough," I declared. "I'm not. No one is. But if the Father says he will give good gifts to his children, you are one of his children, entitled to a good gift. The Holy Spirit wants to be your helper, teacher, and encourager. And he wants to pray through you. Now, just ask him sometime when you're alone."

"OK, I'll do it," she said. A short time later Lib and her husband Gene were in church on Wednesday night, listening to their pastor's message. Suddenly the Holy Spirit moved upon both of them at the same time, and they began weeping. As they yielded to the Holy Spirit, they each received their prayer language.

After that, Lib and I began to pray together on the phone every weekday morning at 8:00, for five minutes. Our focus: to pray for our children. How glad I was that both my husband and my best friend were now enjoying the fullness of the Spirit. Lib and I were prayer partners for years to come.

Rest and Release

Soon after receiving the baptism of the Holy Spirit, I got a copy of John Sherrill's book, *They Speak with Other Tongues*. I devoured it. Few books were available in those days to explain how the Holy Spirit was changing the lives of contemporary Christians. Because he was a member of a mainline denomination, I respected what he said. I gave away copies by the dozens.

In Sherrill's book I read testimonies of those whom he had interviewed and asked, "What is the *use* of speaking in tongues?" A housewife's response: "What's the use of a blue-bird? What is the use of a sunset? Just sheer unmitigated uplift, just joy unspeakable and with it health and peace and rest and release from burdens and tension."[1]

A minister told him how he was able to rest while traveling: "The minute I close my eyes I begin to pray in the Spirit. I pray all night that way, waking up and drifting back to sleep, always praying. I don't get much sleep, but I get a lot of rest. The next morning I'm fresh and strong and ready for a full day's work."[2]

After that, whenever I'd wake up at night, I would pray in tongues, just like that minister, and found I also awoke very refreshed. I knew two things were happening when I prayed this way: First, I was building myself up in the Holy Spirit (see Jude 20); and second, some of the time I was interceding in the Spirit for others (see Rom 8:27).

Sherrill's book encouraged me, because he'd approached the subject as a reporter and ended up receiving the baptism of the Holy Spirit himself. From his many interviews with those who had this experience he came to a conclusion:

Of all the variety of experience with the Holy Spirit, one thing held true in every case. Whether the Baptism came quietly or with a bang, unexpectedly or after long seeking, the ultimate result was to draw the individual closer to Christ. Jesus was no longer a figure on the pages of a history book. Nor, even a memory from some personal mountain-top experience. His Spirit was with the Baptized believer in a present-time, minute-by-minute way, showing him at every turn the nature and personality of Christ.[3]

How Do We Respond to This Gift?

The Holy Spirit can be described in many ways, but he is repeatedly referred to as a *gift*. Furthermore, anyone who accepts Jesus Christ as Savior and asks him for the gift of the Holy Spirit is eligible to receive.

The ways we respond upon receiving this gift are as varied as the Holy Spirit's ways of working in our lives. Katy, whose story we shared in the last chapter, found that the Holy Spirit sustained her with his strength. Several other friends shared with us their feelings and responses when they received the Holy Spirit:

- "I was so wrapped in the love of Jesus, I wanted to stay enfolded in his arms forever," Dorothy told us. "It was like the day I got married, had my first baby placed in my arms, and enjoyed the best Christmas ever—all rolled into one. I wanted to rush up and down my street, telling everyone about Jesus, the Lord of my life."

- Rex knew he needed the power of the Holy Spirit in his life because he continued to struggle with temptation and the effects of the "sinful baggage" from his past as a gangster and drug dealer. When his spiritual mother prayed for him to be filled with the Holy Spirit, a deep sense of his love for God and of God's love for him welled up in his heart.

"Several days later I was on my knees just worshipping Jesus for saving the likes of me," Rex said. "As I ran out of words, suddenly a beautiful language started pouring out of my mouth. I knew I was worshipping the Lord in prayer, but by faith I had to choose to move my mouth and allow the heavenly language to come out. As I have grown over the past twenty-five years, I have never stopped exercising the gift of prayer through the Holy Spirit, and he has given me boldness in sharing my experiences with Jesus. I believe the true sign of this fresh filling of God must be a deeper, more transparent love for Jesus. His love is always the primary key."

- After Craig accepted the Lord in the midst of an emotional crisis, he had a great hunger to know God more intimately. He began attending church and would go to the altar to ask for prayer to draw closer to the Lord. But the pastor responded by trying to sign him up to drive a Sunday school bus. Then while training for his night-shift restaurant job, Craig met a Christian coworker, Otto, who told him about the Holy Spirit and invited him to a house prayer meeting. When he left that meeting to go to work, Craig knew he wanted the experience the people had been talking about. That night on the job, while battling with his fear and doubts about speaking in tongues, he was surprised to see his friend Otto walk into the restaurant. "The Lord showed me that you're having a struggle," he said. "So I came to answer your questions about the Holy Spirit and pray with you."

A few weeks later Craig was driving and praying when he

felt God's presence come into the car. "I started weeping as waves of God's love swept over me, and when I began to worship him, it was in a language I'd never learned," Craig said. "My walk with the Lord intensified after that experience, and God restored me completely from the effects of years of drug abuse."

- Ceci received the Holy Spirit at age fourteen, and it completely changed her life. "I had an intense hunger for the Bible—I couldn't get enough," she said. "I led many classmates to the Lord and matured beyond my years in Bible knowledge. Mom wasn't sure what to make of this, so she just watched me. But she liked the fruit she saw in my life because I never went into teenage rebellion."

- Lynn's response was musical. "Now when I play the piano I play melodies as the Holy Spirit gives them to me, and sing praises to God in my prayer language," she reported. "This new experience came after I received the baptism in the Holy Spirit."

- Kay, who had suffered abuse as a child and really never knew what it was like to be loved, had decided that living the Christian life was just too difficult. She was ready to give up. At one point in her struggle a minister had laid hands on her and prayed for her to receive the Holy Spirit. Four years later, God's presence literally "invaded" her car, and she began speaking in tongues as she was driving. Pulling to the side of the road, Kay prayed in tongues for more than two hours. During that time she felt the Holy Spirit set her free from every bondage that had hindered her walk with the Lord. After returning home, she continued for three days to speak in tongues almost continually.

"I gave up striving to overcome in my own strength," she reported. "Now, as I yield to the Holy Spirit and allow him to work in my heart, I can relax and enjoy his friendship and his presence, knowing I'm loved and accepted by the Father just as I am."

- After being challenged to read the Book of Acts, Diane realized she lacked power. "I see now that the Holy Spirit *is* power," she said. "Praying in tongues has given me boldness to witness to others about the Lord, and enabled me to help deliver those oppressed by unclean spirits. I didn't know it was possible for an ordinary Christian to help set people free from evil, tormenting spirits."

- When Robert saw how the Holy Spirit changed his wife after he'd watched her carefully for several months, he decided he wanted to experience that same closeness to God. He and a friend drove to a church sixty miles away to ask the pastor and lay leaders to pray for him to receive the Holy Spirit. He returned home, believing in faith that he had received, but he didn't have a prayer language. However, the next morning, while commuting to work, he suddenly began praising God with a torrent of words he'd never learned before. From then on he prayed in tongues on the way to work every day.

- Martha had an encounter with the Holy Spirit after reading a book about the beauty of praying in a heavenly language. She had sought the baptism many times—even going off alone to the woods for a time of solitude with the Lord— but had finally concluded, "This experience just isn't for me, because I've asked and nothing has happened." That night she got on her knees and began her prayer by saying, "Oh, God...," when suddenly she heard herself utter five strange syllables. "I won't think about this anymore," she said to herself, startled. "But if I wake up tomorrow and speak these same syllables, I'll know I have tongues." As soon as she awoke the next day, those same syllables came out of her mouth when she began praising God.

"I was overcome with his presence and holiness and knew this was my vehicle for offering praise to God," she said. "For the next five years I looked on the experience only as praise, never knowing I could use this gift to pray for other people, or even pray in tongues and ask God for interpretation. I had been a Christian for fifty years before I experienced the baptism of the Holy Spirit. How I wish I hadn't waited so long—but no one told me about it."

- Gloria, who had been reared an Orthodox Jew, came to Christ after a long period of rebellion against God. Three weeks after her conversion, while reading a book that suggested asking for the baptism of the Holy Spirit, she spontaneously began to speak a phrase in tongues. Her "momma in the Lord" showed her that this occurred in the New Testament during the Jewish Feast of Pentecost, and that her experience was biblical. She continued using her limited prayer language, but a few days later an amazing thing happened.

"Suddenly I broke loose singing in tongues and it was the most glorious Hebrew pouring from my lips I have ever heard," Gloria reported. She could not speak Hebrew, but she recognized it from her years of attending synagogue. "I felt as if I were sitting in the synagogue. My experience of speaking in tongues validated my encounter with Jesus, because all my life I had understood that if one of my people accepted Jesus he was no longer a Jew. But now for the first time since becoming a believer I knew that I was definitely still a Jew! After that, the Word of God really became alive for me."

These experiences are diverse, yet all of these people have several things in common:

- Each had accepted Christ as Savior prior to receiving the Holy Spirit (as in Acts 8:15-17).
- Each felt a need to seek a deeper relationship with the Lord.
- Each person's encounter with the Holy Spirit impacted his or her life according to individual needs and personality traits.

Functions of the Holy Spirit

We find in Scripture that the Holy Spirit's functions in the life of the yielded believer are many and varied, as this list illustrates. The Holy Spirit ...

- confirms our salvation: Romans 8:16; 1 John 3:24; 4:13
- gives life: Romans 8:5-11
- gives joy: Acts 13:52; Romans 14:17
- gives hope: Romans 15:13; 1 Thessalonians 1:6
- liberates: Romans 8:1-2
- gives strength to overcome sin: Romans 8:9-11; Galatians 5:16
- seals our inheritance in Christ: 1 Corinthians 1:22; Ephesians 1:13-14

- speaks through us: Matthew 10:19-20
- teaches: Luke 12:12; John 14:26; 1 Corinthians 2:13
- comforts: John 14:16 (KJV)
- testifies of Jesus: John 15:26; 1 John 5:6
- convicts of sin: John 16:7-8
- speaks and guides: John 16:13; Acts 10:19; 16:6; Romans 8:14
- empowers to witness: Luke 4:14; Acts 1:8; 1 Peter 1:12
- enables to speak with tongues: Acts 2:4; 19:6
- strengthens and encourages: Acts 9:31
- loves through us: Romans 5:5
- produces righteous fruit: Galatians 5:22-23
- helps us pray: Romans 8:26-27; 1 Corinthians 14:15
- helps us worship: Ephesians 5:18-19; Philippians 3:3
- reveals the things of God: 1 Corinthians 2:9-10
- gives spiritual gifts: 1 Corinthians 12:7-11
- edifies our spirits: 1 Corinthians 14:2,4; Ephesians 3:16; Jude 18-20
- unites believers: Philippians 2:1-2; Ephesians 4:3-4

What an extraordinary gift the Father bestowed upon his children when he sent the Holy Spirit to be our helper! Is it any wonder that Satan tries to minimize the significance of the gift and divide and confuse the body of Christ concerning it?

As the Christians we've written about in this chapter have illustrated, each of us has a choice: to believe and receive, or to reject God's gift of the Holy Spirit. If you are among those who long for greater intimacy with the Lord, you may wish to pray the prayer that follows.

Prayer

Lord, I yearn for the Holy Spirit to make a difference in my life. I choose to lay down any preconceived ideas or wrong beliefs I've had concerning the indwelling of the Holy Spirit. Thank you for this wonderful gift. I desire for the Holy Spirit to strengthen me. May I, in turn, allow him to pray through me, comfort through me, teach through me. Lord, invade my life. I invite you to do whatever you wish to do as I wholeheartedly yield to your Spirit. Amen.

THREE

How Do I Receive the Holy Spirit?

If you then, though you are evil, know how to give good gifts to your children, how much more will your Father in heaven give the Holy Spirit to those who ask him!

LUKE 11:13

How can I receive the Holy Spirit?

Perhaps you've been pondering this question as you've been learning more about who the Holy Spirit is and how he makes a difference in our lives. The above Scripture assures us that our heavenly Father delights to give this gift when we ask him. Therefore, asking for the Holy Spirit is a good place to begin.

In this chapter you will meet people whose lives changed dramatically when they asked the Lord to baptize them in the Holy Spirit. Some of these friends were simply seeking a deeper experience with him, and received this gift during their quest. Yet God responded to each individual in a way that he or she could best understand and receive. Mind you, these were not cookie-cutter experiences, but powerful personal encounters with the Holy Spirit.

A Search for Something More

William received a revelation of truth in a most unusual way. He was eighteen years old, stoned on drugs, and headed to a beach in San Diego when God invaded his little Volkswagen and gave him an "open vision." Before his eyes flashed a picture of a black poster with a line going across it and dropping off into an abyss. He had grown up in church, but such a thing had never happened to him before—and this definitely wasn't a drug trip.

"The Lord seemed to say to me that he had a will for my life, but if I didn't turn around right now he couldn't—or wouldn't—help me," William told us. "I knew I was on the verge of falling into that abyss if I didn't change my lifestyle. I quickly sobered up and pulled to the side of the road to surrender my life to God. Then I drove home and found that my mother had been praying for me at that precise time. Only God knows what her prayers saved me from that night."

Two weeks later William went off to a Christian college more than a thousand miles from home. As the semester progressed he tried to seek God more and more, but kept hitting a dead end in getting help to overcome problems from his past. "I knew I needed deliverance and healing because I was still smoking pot and had other habits I wanted to get rid of," he said. "I didn't know where to go for help."

This was the college sponsored by his parents' denomination, which had always taught that the active work of the Holy Spirit ended when the last disciple died. This group believes that now, since we have the Word of God, we don't need the Holy Spirit to function in the same way as recorded in Scripture.

"I knew I needed something more—much more. And I suspected it was the Holy Spirit," William said. "One night I read the entire Book of Acts at one sitting—something I'd never done. By the time I'd finished I was convinced I needed the empowering of the Holy Spirit."

He then went from one teacher to another at this Christian

college, asking for help to overcome the habits with which he continually struggled.

"The teachers said, 'We think it's admirable that you want help or healing, but we don't know what to do,'" William reported. "I knew the Bible said if I'd confess my sins I'd be saved, but the teachers couldn't do anything to help relieve my guilt, or set me free from drugs. One day I burst into the office of the college president and told him I wanted help with my spiritual life. He sent me to the school psychologist, who had me repeat a mantra while staring at a dot on the wall, then read a book on biofeedback. But nothing helped me spiritually or emotionally. The semester ended, and I took a job with some other students, selling Bibles in the backwoods of Alabama."

As he went from door to door, William would ask those who let him into their homes about their philosophy of religion. They all seemed to have a pat answer based on what their particular denomination taught. He and his college-student friends sold Bibles in the daytime and kept up their drug habits at night. Yet William was becoming more and more disgusted with himself because he couldn't find the strength to resist temptation.

One morning as he walked across the Wetumpka River bridge to go to breakfast, he looked down at the murky water below. "I told God I was sick of the guilt and pain I was carrying around, and that I would jump into that river if I didn't think I might go to hell for committing suicide," he said. "I cried out to him for help. My time of selling Bibles was coming to an end, and no one had an answer for me."

Power to Walk in Freedom

Later that day William knocked on the door of a couple who lived far back in the woods. As he pulled out the topical Bible and launched his memorized sales pitch, the potential customer began to ask questions for which the young student wanted answers but lacked the vocabulary even to know how to ask. Not only did the older man ask the questions, however; he also answered them. For three hours he pointed out truths in the Bible and explained the function of the Holy Spirit, assuring William that the power of the Holy Spirit is available today.

As he pondered whether he wanted to know this power, William thought about the fact that he was sure to lose his parents' affirmation. Then he realized, "I've already lost so much— I have nothing more to lose."

He agreed to go outside into the woods with the man for prayer—just the two of them. The older man laid his hands on William and prayed for him to receive the baptism of the Holy Spirit and the gift of tongues, and prophesied over him regarding his future. At first the young student struggled to accept the idea that speaking in tongues actually was legitimate for believers today. Yet before leaving that prayer session, William was praying in an unknown language and was instantly set free from his habits.

Soon after returning to college he began dating Liza, whom he'd met the previous semester, and before long she, too, received the baptism in the Holy Spirit. Today they are married, with two teenage children, and William has his own roofing business. Yet his real passion is evangelism. During his free time you can find him talking to down-and-outers and homeless people in our city, or working in a soup kitchen. He loves sharing his faith with everyone he meets.

"The Holy Spirit directs my steps and my conversation and I allow him to lead me to the people he wants me to talk to," William said. "Sometimes I'm able to bring these people to church, but mainly I just introduce them to my best friend, Jesus. My parents have accepted my experience with the Holy Spirit, because they see that I've truly found freedom from the bondages in my life."

Living by the Spirit

One of the promises Jesus made to his followers about the Holy Spirit was this: "When he, the Spirit of truth, comes, he will guide you into all truth" (Jn 16:13a). Robin and Clark are a young couple who had a life-changing encounter with the Holy Spirit when they sought more of God's presence in their lives. Robin tells the story in her own words:

Both my husband Clark and I were at a time in our lives when we were extremely hungry for God. We were attending an evangelical church, and I was reading and focusing on Romans 8, where it says that we should live according to the Spirit. I wanted to know how to do that, so I went to a Christian bookstore. When I saw *A Woman's Guide to Spirit-Filled Living* [by Quin and Ruthanne] I knew that was the book for me. I brought it home and started reading it that night, looking up every Scripture for myself—even the ones that were printed out in the book. I wanted to see it in *my* Bible. And I prayed the prayers provided at the end of each chapter.

When I read the chapter on receiving the baptism of the Holy Spirit, and looked up the Scriptures to back it up, I did the same as with the other chapters—I prayed the prayer at the end. But when I prayed this time it was different. I began to weep as I felt God's presence. I had a deep desire to worship him, and when I opened my mouth to express my worship, out came a language I didn't know.

Clark had been brought up in a traditional church and had certain opinions about the phenomenon of speaking in tongues. We had talked about this before, but since I hadn't been raised in the church at all, I had no preconceived ideas about the matter. Clark always maintained that speaking in tongues wasn't from God, but occurred because of people getting "carried away" emotionally. So I didn't tell him that I was baptized in the Holy Spirit. I knew how he felt about it, and out of respect for him, I would always wait until I was alone to pray in tongues.

One afternoon when Clark was at home to watch the children, I wanted some quiet time alone with the Lord. Our house was on a one-acre lot, so I told my husband I was going out to the back of the property to enjoy the sunshine and spend some time with God. I went outside and began praying in the Spirit. But it so happened that I had unwittingly chosen a spot from which sound traveled directly to the house—of all spots to pick!

When Clark heard me making these strange sounds he came outside to see if I was OK, thinking something must be terribly wrong. But I had my eyes closed and didn't see him. When I became aware that he was there and opened my eyes, he just started to walk away without saying anything.

Then an amazing thing happened—something that has never occurred again since that day. I tried to explain to Clark what had happened to me, but I couldn't say anything in English. Only tongues would come out. I followed him to the house, but could speak only in tongues for the next ten minutes or so. It made me laugh because it was so strange. No matter what I tried to say, it would come out in tongues. After a few minutes, Clark started to laugh, too. Finally, when I got my English back, I explained to him about reading the book and what had happened after I had prayed to receive the Holy Spirit.

He was really quiet—I didn't know how he might respond. After a few moments he said, "I know you, and I know you wouldn't do something that wasn't genuine. Can I read the book, too?"

"But it's a *woman's* guide," I reminded him.

"I don't care—I want everything God has for me, regardless of how I get it," he said.

"Just make sure none of the guys at work see you reading a *woman's* guide to anything!" I told him jokingly.

So he read the book and checked out all the Bible verses, just as I had done. One day while I was out with a friend, he prayed the same prayer at the end of the chapter that I had prayed. When I got home he came out of the bedroom looking slightly dazed.

"Are there flames of fire on my head?" he asked. He was quite serious in asking the question, and he clearly expected me to say "yes."

"No, there are no flames of fire on your head," I said, laughing.

He told me that he had knelt down beside the bed and told God he wanted everything he had to give. Then he prayed to receive the Holy Spirit. He said he felt a heat that started at the top of his head, moved down his face, flowed down until it reached his mouth, and then he began speaking in tongues. The sensation was so strong, he thought surely there must have been literal flames on his head!

After that, we took the advice in the book to get a mature mentor to help us, and we rapidly grew in our faith. We stayed in the same church and began getting more involved because we felt serving there was where we belonged. But we would attend a charismatic church on Sunday evenings for what we called our "feeding time." One of our pastors called us aside once and asked us what was going on—he had noticed a change in us. We told him that we had been baptized in the Holy Spirit.

Later we felt God calling Clark to leave the job he'd had for fifteen years at an automotive design company to go to Bible school and prepare for ministry. We both graduated from Christ for the Nations Institute in Dallas, and have completed a year of pastoral internship at a church in Michigan. Soon we'll be going to Spain to be administrators at a Bible school there.

Since receiving the Holy Spirit, I don't feel that I'm the same person I used to be. I feel the presence of God, and I have a fire and passion that is deeper and stronger than the hunger I once felt. At the time I bought that book, I was a smoker, although I had tried and tried to quit. After I was baptized in the Holy Spirit, I asked him to give me the strength and power to overcome this habit. Every time I was tempted to smoke, I asked the Holy Spirit to help me, and he did, until the temptations were gone completely, and I haven't smoked since.

I have been healed in many areas of my heart because of feeling his love and strength in a real and present way. Since the day I was baptized in the Holy Spirit, I both *feel* and *know* that God is with me.

Clark himself reports on the effects of his own experience:

The Holy Spirit has changed me quite drastically. I am definitely not the same person I was before. In fact, someone who knew me well on my former job could not believe the change in me when he saw me for the first time in four years. There is a boldness in me that I never had before. Previously I was a quiet person who could not even pray aloud in front of another person, let alone try to witness to anyone. Now I am able to share the gospel boldly, give my testimony, and pray for those God leads me to. I've had the opportunity to lead people to Christ and the baptism of the Holy Spirit in a state penitentiary. I've helped present the gospel in drama to crowds of fifteen thousand in India, and reached out to people in the streets of Geneva, Switzerland, with the love of Christ. Although I was raised in a Christian home, there was always something missing. I always sensed a hunger to know God better, to be closer to him. That "missing something" was found when I received the baptism of the Holy Spirit.

Robin and Clark's story illustrates how faithful the Holy Spirit is to reveal the reality of his power to those who diligently seek him. In other cases, a crisis may be the means God uses to draw a person to know him more intimately. This doesn't mean that it was God's will for a tragedy to occur, yet the Holy Spirit does work in the midst of adversity, and can bring blessing out of it in amazing ways.

Spiritual Hunger Satisfied

Hilda had gone to church all her life, because her parents had instilled that habit in her, and she was raising her own four children the same way. She loved God and never missed a church service, but she had no knowledge of how to walk close to the Lord on a daily basis. Then crisis struck.

A serious boating accident mutilated Hilda's face, requiring numerous surgeries and a long convalescence. Since she couldn't attend church or pursue any activities, she began reading one Christian book after another. It was then that God began dealing with her anemic spiritual life.

"After four months of recovery, I was again able to attend church, but all the reading I had done caused me to feel dissatisfied," she said. "Then I read the book *Nine O'Clock in the Morning* by Father Dennis Bennett and learned how God met this Episcopal priest's discontentment by giving him an experience he described as the baptism of the Holy Spirit. His book planted a seed in my heart as I discovered there was much more to the Christian life than I had known. I realized that anyone—including a homemaker like me—could ask the Holy Spirit to baptize her. I became a seeker after all God had for me."

One evening when Hilda attended a church service and the invitation was given, she asked the pastor if she could share something with the congregation. She stood and told the people that through the ordeal of her accident, she had found a new walk with the Lord.

"The doctors put the bones back into my face, but it was God who made them grow back together and heal," she said. "It took this accident to teach me that I had to totally surrender to him—to really know him. What I'm trying to say is, God still heals today."

Then Hilda knelt on the platform and began to pray. Suddenly everyone in the congregation came forward and knelt before the Lord, some crying, some repenting. Afterward, when several couples went to Hilda's home for fellowship, all she could do was raise her hands and say, "Isn't the Lord wonderful!"

"I don't think any of them understood this new love I had for God," she told us. "Later that night, after everyone had left and my family had gone to bed, I felt a nudge from the Lord to go into my den, where I like to pray. As I began to praise him I said, 'Lord, these words just do not adequately express the way I feel about you.' Then suddenly I began to pray in an unknown tongue. I felt so free and wonderful as joy overcame me, filling the inner void I'd become aware of. I had surely been baptized with the Holy Spirit.

"This began a new walk with my Savior that I never thought possible. The Holy Spirit has helped me to understand the Bible more clearly and enabled me to teach many Bible studies in these ensuing years. I have prayed for literally dozens of people to receive the baptism of the Holy Spirit, and have seen their lives change just as mine did. I guess it took a crisis to turn me around. I'm just so grateful that during my time of convalescence I found the answer to my spiritual hunger."

In case after case, those who shared their experiences with us discovered the power of the Holy Spirit as they sought a closer relationship with the Lord. For most of them, the experience of speaking in tongues came as they expressed their worship to him. We see this common thread in the following story.

Power to Pray More Fervently

In Linda we meet another "seeker" who found the answers to her questions as she wholeheartedly searched the New Testament for truth.

Linda had been a Christian for more than twenty years, and did her best to pray for issues her pastor presented to the congregation for prayer each week. Yet, sensing that something was missing, she began to read the New Testament with new interest, asking God to reveal meanings she might have previously overlooked or misinterpreted.

As she read through the Book of Acts, Linda was amazed to see how many times the Holy Spirit made a difference in the lives of the early church believers. She knew that her denomination took a strong stand against speaking in tongues, yet she kept reading about it in the Bible.

"Don't I, too, need this power to pray more effectively? To live a life closer to the Lord?" she asked herself. Questions plagued her as she read several translations of Scripture, using a concordance to help her find cross-references to the Holy Spirit. Soon she came to the conclusion that God indeed had *not* limited the gift of the Holy Spirit and speaking in tongues to only the early church. She could ask for this gift herself.

One day, alone in her bedroom, Linda placed her Bible on the bed and knelt with childlike faith to pray. "Lord, I believe you desire to fill me with the Holy Spirit. I am asking you to do that, and believing you will. I will open my mouth and speak with new tongues, just as your followers did on the day of Pentecost. Thank you, Lord."

In moments a torrent of words came from her mouth—words of praise to God, she was sure—but in a language she had never learned.

"My first response was to sense an overwhelming love for Jesus Christ and a joy I'd never felt before," Linda said. "I was aware of a strength I'd never encountered before—especially the power to pray. When I received a prayer language, my prayer life changed dramatically. Not only do I pray more 'with understanding,' I also pray in tongues almost constantly while doing menial tasks. I feel I enter into praise and worship on a higher level. In my private prayer time, when I don't know how or what to pray for those on my prayer list, I pray in tongues for them."

As we see in these seekers' stories, many believers deprive themselves of the fullness of the Spirit because they feel the issue is too controversial, or because they're afraid of speaking in tongues. Yet if Jesus speaks of the Holy Spirit as being a "good gift" (Lk 11:13), we should desire to receive it, rather than rob ourselves of the blessing.

In his book *Living the Spirit-Formed Life*, Pastor Jack Hayford points out the relationship between speaking in tongues and a spirit of praise and worship. "It's often debated as to whether speaking with tongues is or isn't a sign of being filled with the Holy Spirit," he says. "I do believe the Word of God makes it clear that this language of praise is a dynamic *privilege* available to people who are filled with the Spirit."[1]

Most people you speak to about their own such experience will tell you, "Since being baptized in the Holy Spirit, my times of praise and worship and prayer have become more intense and more meaningful."

Have You Received?

Have you received the Holy Spirit since you believed?

Paul asked this of the believers at Ephesus, and learned that they were ignorant about the Holy Spirit. Yet, "when Paul placed his hands on them, the Holy Spirit came on them, and they spoke in tongues and prophesied" (Acts 19:6).

The battleground is in our minds, as the enemy will do anything to stop us from receiving the gifts of the Holy Spirit. Some people get psychological, analytical, or legalistic about the experience. Others fear intimidation and opposition from family or friends, or fear they will do something that will make them appear foolish. Ignorance, lack of understanding, and spiritual pride are factors that hold many people back from receiving God's gifts.

Hundreds of seekers received the Holy Spirit through the ministry of the late Gordon Lindsay, founder of Christ for the Nations, especially during the late 1960s and early 1970s. He provides this helpful advice:

> As most of us know, the tongue is the most difficult member of the body to control. It is usually the last member for the Holy Spirit to conquer. Even when the person begins to speak in other tongues, he may unconsciously resist the Holy Spirit and revert back to speaking in his familiar vernacular. But if the person is reassured and encouraged to yield his tongue to these unfamiliar sounds, there will come forth a few inarticulate words or phrases that are often repeated, and then different words, and finally sentences. Invariably, these words are languages unknown to the person. When heard by one who knows the language, or has the gift of interpretation, they are found to be words of praise and adoration to God. Sometimes a person newly baptized will preach a short sermon or give an exhortation in the unknown tongue.
>
> ... It is not surprising that we have to encourage and

even persuade people to yield their tongues to Him. Although the Spirit of God has all power, He is mild and gentle and compels none. The Spirit leads men, but never drives. He guides into truth, but never forces.[2]

It seems quite clear from Scripture that the Holy Spirit desires to completely indwell every believer. Yet he is not pushy—he waits for an invitation. If you hunger for more of God, we urge you to follow the guidelines below, then pray a prayer similar to the one Quin prayed that night in the pastor's study, and open your heart to receive all he desires to give you.

Basic Steps to Follow

1. Confess and repent of any sin in your life. Forgive anyone who has ever hurt you, disappointed you, or falsely accused you. Ask the Lord to remind you of any resentment you may be harboring, and release it through prayer (read Mk 11:22-26 and Eph 4:25-32).
2. Ask the Lord to reveal to you any involvement you may have had with the occult (read Dt 7:25-26; 18:10-12; Acts 19:19-20). Repent and ask forgiveness, no matter how naive you may have been when you participated in any occult activity. Receive God's forgiveness, then renounce the devil and all his works in your life.
3. If you have ever mocked or made fun of anyone who spoke in tongues—even in casual joking—ask God to forgive you for not honoring the Holy Spirit.
4. Ask for the infilling of the Holy Spirit, with the ability to pray in tongues. Then open your mouth and begin to speak the syllables the Holy Spirit gives you to say. Your lips may begin

to tremble or your tongue to stammer, but don't be fearful—just begin to speak out the sounds, though they may seem strange to you. One of the best ways to receive is through singing. Many receive their prayer language by beginning to sing the simple chorus, "Hallelujah, Hallelujah, Hallelujah ..." and then singing syllables to that tune as the Holy Spirit enables them.

5. Use your prayer language every day. It helps you to stay close to the Lord and strengthens your spiritual life. As you exercise this gift you will become less and less self-conscious and more fluent in your prayer language, and your vocabulary will increase. Remember, you cannot pray in your natural language and your new prayer language at the same time.

6. Ask God to lead you to a Spirit-filled prayer partner to pray with you on a regular basis. It should be a friend of the same sex, or your spouse. Praying with like-minded friends will encourage you and build your faith as you see your prayers answered.

Perhaps you once experienced the reality of the Holy Spirit, but you've grown complacent and lukewarm in your Spirit-filled walk. We challenge you—as Paul did Timothy—to "stir up the gift of God which is in you" (2 Tm 1:6, NKJV). We pray that the Holy Spirit will become as real to you as your best friend. May you begin to experience sweet fellowship with him on a regular basis.

Prayer

Heavenly Father, I acknowledge that Jesus Christ is my Lord and Savior. Thank you for the wonderful gift of the Holy Spirit. I confess to you my sin of (*unbelief, unforgiveness, pride, selfishness ...*) and ask for your forgiveness and cleansing.

Lord, please reveal any involvement with false religions or occultic activity in my life (*pause and allow time for God's revelation to come to you*). I renounce any such sin (*name witchcraft, astrology, use of a Ouija board, fortune-telling, or whatever God has revealed*), and ask you to forgive me.

Forgive me, Lord, for ever ridiculing things of the Holy Spirit. I acknowledge my need to receive this gift in greater measure. Help me to lay aside my prejudices and preconceived ideas about the work of the Holy Spirit, and receive all that you have for me.

Lord, I open my mouth to speak, and fully yield my will to you to allow the Holy Spirit to speak through me. I expect the Holy Spirit to give me a new tongue. By faith, I will worship you in that new language. . . .

FOUR

Why Speak in Tongues?

When the day of Pentecost came, they were all together in one place. Suddenly a sound like the blowing of a violent wind came from heaven and filled the whole house where they were sitting. They saw what seemed to be tongues of fire that separated and came to rest on each of them. All of them were filled with the Holy Spirit and began to speak in other tongues as the Spirit enabled them.

ACTS 2:1-4

It must have been an awesome experience!

Imagine being one of the 120 people sitting quietly in the Upper Room when the sound of a tornado-force wind swept into the place, followed by what appeared to be flames of fire resting on each person's head. It was the ultimate "sound and light show" to announce the gift of the Holy Spirit, which Jesus had promised the Father would send. Then, simultaneously, they all began speaking praises to God in languages they had never learned.

Nothing like this had ever happened before in the history of God's people—it is a phenomenon unique to New Testament believers. Other supernatural manifestations had occurred throughout Old Testament times and during the earthly ministry of Christ. Yet on this day, when the Holy Spirit came, a new era began for the church.

The unusual sounds drew a large crowd of people who had

come to the temple in Jerusalem from many nations to observe the Feast of Pentecost. Perplexed to hear their own languages being spoken by these uneducated people from Galilee, many of them asked, "What does this mean?" Some mocked, saying they'd had too much wine.

Then Peter stood up and explained that the Holy Spirit had been poured out, as Jesus had promised. At the end of his speech he declared, "Repent and be baptized, every one of you, in the name of Jesus Christ for the forgiveness of your sins. And you will receive the gift of the Holy Spirit. The promise is for you and your children and for all who are far off—for all whom the Lord our God will call" (Acts 2:38-39).

Receiving the Holy Spirit Is Biblical

Three thousand people responded to Peter's message that day and were baptized. Today, more than two thousand years later, believers are still included in the "all who are far off" category to receive the promised Holy Spirit. Every follower of Christ is eligible.

Let's review the Scriptures that teach us the validity of receiving the Holy Spirit and speaking in tongues:

- The sending of the Holy Spirit was the fulfillment of Old Testament prophecy (Is 28:11-12; 1 Cor 14:21).
- Jesus told his followers that one sign that would accompany the baptism of the Holy Spirit would be that "they will speak in new tongues" (Mk 16:17).
- Jesus promised the indwelling presence of the Holy Spirit to be with us forever (Jn 14:15-17).

- He declared that his followers would receive power when the Holy Spirit came upon them, and that they would be his witnesses to the ends of the earth (Lk 24:49; Acts 1:8).

- The apostles laid hands on the new believers of Samaria to receive the Holy Spirit, because they had been baptized only in the name of the Lord Jesus, in response to Philip's preaching (Acts 8:14-17).

- God sent Ananias to lay hands on Saul (later renamed Paul) that he might be filled with the Holy Spirit (Acts 9:17).

- While Peter was speaking to the household of Cornelius, the Holy Spirit came upon all of them and they spoke in tongues and praised God (Acts 10:44-46). This was the first time non-Jewish believers had received the gift of the Holy Spirit.

- When Paul laid hands on twelve believers in Ephesus, the Holy Spirit came upon them and they spoke in tongues and prophesied (Acts 19:1-6).

- When we don't know what to pray for, Scripture assures us that the Holy Spirit intercedes for us according to God's will, with "groans that words cannot express" (Romans 8:26-27).

- The believer who speaks in tongues edifies (that is, strengthens) him- or herself spiritually (1 Cor 14:4; Jude 20).

- Paul desired every believer to speak in tongues, and said, "I thank God that I speak in tongues more than all of you" (1 Cor 14:5, 18).

- Paul acknowledged the value of praying and singing in tongues in his own experience (1 Cor 14:13-15).

- Tongues are a sign for unbelievers (1 Cor 14:22).

- Speaking in tongues should not be forbidden (1 Cor 14:39).

- We should pray in the Holy Spirit "on all occasions with all kinds of prayers and requests" (Eph 6:18).

Overcoming Prejudice

Gene is an example of a typical businessman who, though raised in the church, had closed his mind to anything other than what he'd always been taught in his denomination. His wife, Pam, had attended a renewal service and received the baptism of the Holy Spirit, but he, at age thirty-one, was well satisfied with his spiritual life and saw no reason to change in any way. When Pam told him about her new love for Christ, Gene would repeat over and over to her the verse that had been drilled into him at his church. "One baptism—only one baptism," he would tell her (based upon Eph 4:5).

She responded by quietly praying that he would open his heart, but she never pressured him. Once in a while he would attend meetings with Pam where he saw the outpouring of God's power—healings, deliverances, and speaking in tongues. Frankly, that kind of power scared him, but he couldn't deny that God was performing miracles just like those recorded in the Book of Acts. Finally, when he started attending businessmen's dinners where ordinary men like himself shared about God doing miraculous things in their lives, he grew hungry to know more.

Pam and Gene had bought a Christian retreat center, which they operated on weekends, while he continued his manufacturing job during the week. One weekend when Pam had gone home early, Gene stayed late with a group of young people who were working at the center. That evening, he asked some of them to pray for him to receive the Holy Spirit. "Just receive in faith," one young man told him. When the group prayed with him, Gene truly believed that God touched him, although nothing unusual happened. However, about eleven o'clock that night, while driving home with his ten-year-old daughter asleep on the seat beside him, he had an encounter with God.

"All I can say is the power of God entered the car," he reported. "It was like waves of electricity washing over me. I started trembling, then began to speak in tongues. My life was changed dramatically in a moment's time. I received new understanding of the Bible as it opened up to me in a totally new light, and I had a deeper compassion for people. Since then I have prayed for many people to receive the baptism of the Holy Spirit and seen their lives changed. Now I am semiretired from my manufacturing job and spend most of my time in ministry work. My wife and I lead several Bible studies, are mentoring younger couples, and frequently lead retreats. I could never have done this without the infilling of the Holy Spirit."

As is the case for most believers we have interviewed, Gene and Pam speak in tongues primarily in their private prayer times for worship and intercession. They feel this makes their worship experience more meaningful, and their intercession more effective.

Speaking in tongues "is practiced devotionally by the believer in his most intimate and intercessory moments of communication with God as he is moved upon by the Holy Spirit," writes commentator Paul Walker. He also says that "speaking with tongues is a properly expected sign, affirming the Holy Spirit's abiding presence and assuring the believer of an invigorated living witness."[1]

The Value of the Gift of Tongues

The apostle Paul considered speaking in tongues to be important and desirable for the believer, as revealed in these verses he wrote to the church at Corinth:

> I would like every one of you to speak in tongues.... I thank God that I speak in tongues more than all of you.
>
> 1 CORINTHIANS 14:5, 18

A well-respected seminary professor, who questioned the belief that speaking in tongues is legitimate for believers today, struggled to understand why Paul placed such a high value on this practice. Finally, after extensive research and study, he changed his skeptical point of view, received the Holy Spirit, and began to speak in tongues. In his book, *Surprised by the Power of the Spirit*, Jack Deere writes:

> How could this man who was burdened with so much responsibility spend more time than anyone else speaking in tongues? He could only do so if he found the gift of tongues immensely valuable in cultivating his spiritual life and intimacy with God. Indeed, this is precisely what Paul claimed for the gift of tongues when he said, "He who speaks in a tongue edifies himself" (1 Cor 14:4). That is why he wished all Christians had that gift. Does that sound like the attitude of someone who thought tongues were of temporary value to the church? . . . Paul is writing under the inspiration of the Holy Spirit. He is giving us not just his opinion but God's opinion of the gift of tongues. I could not find one other example in Paul's writings where

he placed such a high value on something that was supposedly limited to the first century.[2]

Does the Holy Spirit Cause Division?

Sometimes doctrinal differences may be so strong that they cause family members to suffer division, or, as in the following example, separate a couple who had planned to marry.

Audrey had received the baptism of the Holy Spirit as a young girl and had never wavered in her walk with the Lord. She was faithful in her daily Bible study and prayed often. Her boyfriend, Ben, was a Christian but strongly disagreed with Audrey's belief in the power of the Holy Spirit for today.

At first their differences didn't matter to Audrey. They had so many other things in common, especially their love for music. He played the piano, she sang, and they performed together on their college campus and at local churches on weekends. They shared their dreams and hopes for the future, often discussing marriage. As they got acquainted with one another's families, Audrey was troubled when she learned that Ben's parents had the same strong stand against the baptism of the Holy Spirit as he did.

Finally, she realized she could not live in a marriage where her beliefs about the Holy Spirit were questioned and devalued. Ben even pressed her to lay down her beliefs. It was a painful decision, but Audrey knew she had to give up her dreams with this wonderful young man, whom she loved deeply. In obedience to the Lord, she ended the relationship just before her last year of college. "Lord, fill the emptiness in my life," she prayed through her tears during that year—the most painful she had ever endured.

After graduating, Audrey moved as far away from campus as she could get, taking a teaching job at a Christian school. One day, Rick, a young man involved in the music ministry at the church she was attending, spotted her in the congregation. After the service he made haste to introduce himself. First they became friends, and then their relationship blossomed. Within a few months, Rick assured Audrey that he loved her just as she was. He didn't try to change her beliefs in any way. He had received the baptism of the Holy Spirit some years earlier, prayed in tongues, and also was gifted musically.

"I had to wait for God's perfect plan for me, and the man of his choosing," she said. "The Lord required me to trust him for a better way when I gave up Ben. I could not compromise my beliefs and the sweet presence and power of the Holy Spirit." After their marriage, Rick and Audrey moved overseas to serve as missionaries, where God has opened many doors of ministry to them. How glad she is that she made the right decision, despite her heartache at the time.

The Holy Spirit Transcends Our Understanding

Pastor Judson Cornwall provides a clear explanation of the value of praying in tongues:

> Prayer is the most valuable use of tongues for it is "speaking to God." It has been charged that speaking with tongues is gibberish, or, at best, an artificial language, but the Scriptures refer to the language as the "tongues of men and of angels" (1 Cor 13:1). The Holy Spirit is certainly not limited to the English language, nor is He confined to modern languages. He has access to every language

ever used by mankind, and He is very familiar with the language used in heaven. When deep intercession is needed, the Spirit often uses a language that is beyond the intellectual grasp of the speaker to bypass the censorship of his or her conscious mind, thereby enabling the Spirit to say what needs to be prayed without arguing with the faith level of the one through whom the intercession flows.

Praying in tongues is not the work of the subconscious. It's really *supra-intellectual* praying. That is, the prayer is beyond the natural mind, not beneath the conscious level. Intercessory prayer in tongues is not incoherent speech. The very words are motivated by the Holy Spirit, addressed to the Father and approved by the Lord Jesus (see Mk 16:17).[3]

Smith Wigglesworth (1859-1947) once told a story about his friend William Burton (1886-1971), a missionary to Central Africa, who was stricken with illness while in Africa and not expected to live. His coworkers stood around his seemingly lifeless body, brokenhearted. "In a moment, without any signal, he stood in the midst of them," Wigglesworth reported. "They could not understand it. He told them that he came to himself feeling a warmth through his body.... He rose, perfectly healed."

Some time later, when William Burton was speaking at a meeting in London, he told the people how he had been left for dead, but then suddenly was raised up. A lady came to him afterward and asked, "Do you keep a diary?"

When he said that he did, she told him, "One day I went to pray, and as soon as I knelt down you came to my mind. The Spirit of the Lord took hold of me and prayed through me in an unknown tongue. A vision came and I saw you laid out helpless. I cried out in the tongue till I saw you rise up and go out of that room."

He turned to his diary and found it was exactly the date he had been healed.[4]

Examples of Speaking in Tongues

In his extensive teaching about the Holy Spirit, Paul wrote that "anyone who speaks in a tongue does not speak to men but to God. Indeed, no one understands him; he utters mysteries with his spirit" (1 Cor 14:2). This reinforces the idea that speaking in tongues is for one's private prayer time. However, Scripture also provides the following instructions for the use of tongues in public worship settings:

> When you come together, everyone has a hymn, or a word of instruction, a revelation, a tongue or an interpretation. All of these must be done for the strengthening of the church. If anyone speaks in a tongue, two—or at the most three—should speak, one at a time, and someone must interpret. If there is no interpreter, the speaker should keep quiet in the church and speak to himself and God.... But everything should be done in a fitting and orderly way.
>
> 1 CORINTHIANS 14:26-28, 40

Both of us (Quin and Ruthanne) have been in services where an individual gave an utterance in tongues, and someone else provided the interpretation. Sometimes both the utterance in tongues and the interpretation have been given by the same person. In Paul's teaching in 1 Corinthians 14 he addresses the lack of understanding about the difference between speaking in tongues privately and in a public worship service. No restraints are placed upon the private use of tongues, but for believers wanting to speak in tongues in public meetings, Paul gave the above instructions for maintaining order.

I (Quin) remember one of the first times I was in a service where I heard tongues and an interpretation. A Chinese woman sitting behind me spoke in tongues in what sounded to me like Hebrew. A man sitting across the auditorium gave the interpretation, which in essence was an appeal to pray for the Jews and for the city of Jerusalem. The pastor immediately led the congregation in a prayer for the protection of those living in Jerusalem. For days afterward I wondered about what impact our prayers might have had that evening. I now realize the importance of obeying the Holy Spirit's call to pray in a case like this, whether or not we ever hear the end result of the matter.

Sometimes when a person speaks in tongues, one or more persons in the audience may understand what is being said, even though the speaker is using a language he has never learned.

For example, my (Ruthanne's) husband, John, was with a group of believers praying at a church in Kansas one evening, shortly after he had returned from serving as a missionary in South Africa for five years. Suddenly he heard a lady in the group praising God in Zulu (a tribal language he had studied while working among the gold miners in Johannesburg). The woman he heard praying in another tongue was the wife of a wheat farmer, and they spoke only English. Yet in perfect Zulu she was saying over and over, "I praise you, Father."

Years later, John was praying with a pastor in France and heard him praising God in Afrikaans, another language my husband had learned that is spoken only in South Africa. The pastor had never been outside France, and knew no language other than his native tongue.

John's uncle, A.N. Trotter, was a missionary evangelist working in Sierra Leone, West Africa, when he had an even more amazing experience. He was preaching through an interpreter, and invited people to come forward to receive Christ. After leading them in a prayer for salvation, he told them about the baptism with the Holy Spirit and began praying for them to receive as he walked among the crowd. Suddenly he heard a tribal woman expressing praises to God in perfect Oxford English. Everyone around her seemed terribly excited, and Uncle Al couldn't understand why. He asked his interpreter, "Has this woman ever spoken English before?" The man said, "No—in fact, she has never spoken in her life—she is mute!"

Strengthened in the Spirit

Praying in tongues has another benefit. When we pray in the Holy Spirit, we are building up our faith. It is for self-edification (see 1 Cor 14:4). "But you, beloved, building yourselves up on your most holy faith, praying in the Holy Spirit, keep yourselves in the love of God" (Jude 20-21a, NKJV). In other words, praying in the Spirit is not only a means of intercession for others but a means of personally receiving strength from the Holy Spirit. Corrie ten Boom once shared an example from the life of a gospel worker who suffered persecution:

A missionary in China had to endure brainwashing. He resisted and fought against it, but the moment came when he felt he was at the end of his strength. Then he started to pray in tongues. That fellowship with the Lord, in absolute relaxation, was his salvation. The enemy could not influence his mind any longer. I believe that the Lord has given this gift at this time to many of His children in many different churches and groups, because it is a strong weapon and will prove to be so in the final battle. It is a fact that nothing has received so much criticism and opposition, even among believing Christians, as has this gift, which is described so clearly in the Word of God. Paul says in 1 Corinthians 14:5 (PHILLIPS): "I should indeed like you all to speak in tongues."

The "God is dead" theology and occultism, which are practiced even by Christians, receive less criticism and resistance, yes, and even enmity, than this gift from the Spirit.[5]

The Holy Spirit Speaks

My (Ruthanne's) father-in-law, Henry Garlock, went as a pioneer missionary to the unevangelized interior of Liberia, West Africa, in 1920. He had received the Holy Spirit in 1913, then attended Bible school and volunteered for service in Africa. Many miraculous signs accompanied his ministry there, but one remarkable incident involved speaking in tongues.

He had hired porters to trek to the coast to buy food and supplies for the mission station, but en route one of the porters was captured and severely beaten by an enemy tribe of cannibals. He faced certain death. Others in the party escaped and brought word to Henry. When he went to rescue the man, the tribal leaders, enraged by his interference in their affairs, captured him also. The obvious intent was to kill and eat both men—the tribe's way of expressing utter contempt for an enemy. Before killing Henry, however, the witch doctor laid his wand at the captive's feet, indicating that he could now speak in his own defense. The problem was, Henry could not speak the language of this tribe, nor could the worker who had accompanied him. Here is the story, in his own words:

> Suddenly, I began to shake. This disturbed me, as I did not want the people to know how frightened I really was. Then I realized the Holy Spirit had come upon me and the words of Jesus in Mark 13:11 came to me: "Take no thought beforehand what ye shall speak ... but whatsoever shall be given you in that hour, that speak ye: for it is not ye that speak, but the Holy Ghost."
>
> Now, under the anointing of the Spirit, I stood up. I reached down and picked up the witch doctor's wand, which he had laid at my feet. I opened my mouth and began by saying, "Ny lay ..." meaning, "Listen to me." And then it happened. The Holy Spirit took complete control of my tongue and vocal organs, and there poured from my lips a torrent of words that I had never learned. I did not know what I said, nor how long I spoke. But when I had finished, silence reigned.[6]

Not only was Henry's life spared but the tribal leaders told him, "We see that your God has power and fights for you. What can we do to atone for mistreating you?" They prepared food for the entire party, and provided porters to carry the wounded man back to the village from which they had come. In the years since that time, many of Henry's siblings and descendants, including his son, John, also have been involved in missions and other types of Christian ministry.

When all is said and done—reading Scripture, doing research, asking questions—these alone will not cause you to receive the Holy Spirit. You must lay aside your hang-ups and take a leap of faith. In the next chapter we'll examine some of the hang-ups that affect many people.

Prayer

Lord, help me to remember that when I don't know how to pray, the Holy Spirit can pray through me in another tongue as I yield to him. Help me be more alert to your still, small voice calling me to prayer. I want to be more cooperative and yielded. Thank you that this gift of praying in the Spirit also will strengthen me spiritually. How I need that! Again, thank you for loving me enough to send your Holy Spirit. Amen.

FIVE

Are Hang-Ups Holding You Back?

I [Paul] thank God that I speak in tongues more than all
of you. . . . Be eager to prophesy, and do not forbid speaking in tongues.

1 CORINTHIANS 14:18, 39

It's true that this matter of speaking in tongues has become for
many Christians a doctrinal bone of contention. The practice
seems so bizarre and illogical to some that they find it hard to
accept, even when they read it in the Bible. Yet God has ways of
bringing special circumstances into people's lives to bring them
to a place of acceptance.

Fran and Mike are longtime friends of mine (Quin's) who
were led to the Lord by the Dutch evangelist Corrie ten Boom.
For several years Corrie and her traveling companion spent
many restful holidays in Fran and Mike's home.

On one occasion, they visited Corrie at a Christian camp
where she was speaking. As Corrie and Fran were taking a walk
one afternoon, Corrie asked, "Frances, would you like me to
pray for Jesus to baptize you in the Holy Spirit?"

"Yes, I would," Fran replied.

They stopped on the path, then Corrie laid hands on her and
prayed for the Lord Jesus to baptize her with the Holy Spirit.
"Fran, now you can pray in tongues if you wish," Corrie said.

Fran studied her friend's beautiful wrinkled face, then, shaking her head, replied, "I don't wish to." They finished their

walk, returned to the camp dormitory, and Corrie never mentioned the matter of tongues to Fran again.

"The idea of speaking in tongues scared me," Fran later told me. "I was afraid of losing control of my own tongue after a lifetime of being taught to be careful what I say. The idea of someone else speaking through me was frightening. Also, I didn't have a scriptural understanding of tongues. But Corrie never pressured me. Because I didn't 'feel' anything when she prayed, nor immediately thereafter see any significant change in my life, I wasn't really sure whether I had been baptized in the Holy Spirit or not."

A Divine Appointment

A short while later, Fran and Mike were visiting the same church in Destin, Florida, where I had received the Holy Spirit some years earlier. As the pastor finished his message he invited all those who had not been baptized in the Holy Spirit to go to a room behind the sanctuary. There his wife would instruct them and pray for them.

Fran and Mike rather reluctantly went to the back room with the group of seekers. Yet when the pastor's wife mentioned that the gift of tongues is available for believers today, Fran once again hesitated. Following her experience with Corrie at the Christian camp, she had met an evangelist named Chris and heard him teach on the subject. His teaching sounded solid, and she respected him. So she prayed, "Lord, if you want me to speak in tongues, I'll just wait, and if Chris ever comes back to Florida again, I'll have him pray for me."

She had barely breathed her prayer when she looked up to see Chris walk through the door! He had been driving through

Destin, headed for another town, when he felt the Holy Spirit directing him to stop and go into St. Andrews church. He sat down with the congregation, expecting to hear something in the pastor's message to clarify why the Lord had sent him here. Yet he immediately felt led to get up and go down the hall to the last room on the right.

"Fran, Mike, what are you doing here?" he exclaimed, knowing this was not their home church. They were among the few in the room he recognized.

"I guess I was waiting for you," Fran stammered, barely able to speak. "Will you pray for me to receive my prayer language?" He was delighted at the request. When Chris prayed for her, Fran spoke only a few halting words, but he encouraged her to allow the Holy Spirit to continue speaking these words through her during her prayer time. Then he left to carry on with his journey.

The Holy Spirit Praying Through Us

Over the next two months, Fran became more and more fluent as she would pray in tongues for two or three hours a day. Yet, during her prayer time she noticed that the same few syllables were often repeated.

One morning after prayer she turned on the TV just as a talk show host was saying, "We are honored today to have the new president of Egypt with us. Welcome Mr. Anwar Sadat." Fran moved closer to the TV and listened intently as the host again pronounced the Egyptian president's name. She suddenly realized that his was the name she had been saying for the past several weeks while praying in tongues!

"I could feel the hair rise up on my neck," she reported. "I realized God had been directing my prayer as I used my prayer language, and that this man was important to God. I saw that, by way of tongues, the Holy Spirit can pray through yielded believers, thus influencing current world leaders and events those individuals may know nothing about. We have the potential to pray the perfect will of the Father by allowing the Holy Spirit to pray through us."

Fran later prayed for a young woman brought to her home after she had hit a wall while riding a horse. After Fran prayed for her—some of the time in tongues—the young woman, who was studying Spanish in college, said, "You are quoting healing Scriptures in Castillian Spanish. You are saying that by Jesus' stripes, I am healed." She was shocked to know that a prayer language could be a language that she herself understood but that Fran, who was praying, did not know. Because of these experiences, Fran now almost daily prays in tongues for long periods of time as she intercedes for others.[1]

Diversity in Prayer

The apostle Paul gives this instruction regarding prayer:

> Pray in the Spirit on all occasions with all kinds of prayers and requests. With this in mind, be alert and always keep on praying for all the saints.
>
> EPHESIANS 6:18

This verse suggests diversity in prayer—*all kinds*—as well as praying *in the Spirit*, which many believers take to mean praying in tongues. In 1 Corinthians 14:14-15, Paul encourages believers to pray in tongues, but also to pray with their understanding. Fran's testimony illustrates how praying in tongues can lead to dramatic results. Yet, to "pray in the Spirit" also can mean to be specifically led by the Holy Spirit as to how to pray "with your mind" in your own language for a given circumstance.

One summer when I (Ruthanne) was on a month-long ministry trip to France with my husband, I became very ill. Because we were constantly on the move, I didn't try to find a doctor, but asked my husband to pray. I also asked the Holy Spirit to give Cindy, my prayer partner back in Texas, an alert to pray for me.

Upon returning home I called Cindy to tell her how sick I'd been, and that I was better but still struggling with symptoms. "While you were in France, the Lord impressed me to pray specifically for your immune system," she reported. "He didn't pinpoint the problem; I simply prayed as the Holy Spirit directed."

When I went to our family doctor, he put me on strong antibiotics for a kidney infection, and within a couple of weeks I was OK. It was not an instant healing. Yet, I firmly believe Cindy's prayers for my immune system, combined with the prayers of John and other friends, carried me through until I got medical help.

One time in Michigan I was standing at my seat, praying for a woman who had gone forward for prayer during a church meeting. When the Holy Spirit gave me a word of knowledge that she had suffered serious child abuse, I went down and knelt beside her and whispered that in her ear. Then I laid hands on her and began praying in tongues. She told me later, "I don't know what you were saying when you prayed like that, but I felt a healing was taking place deep in my spirit."

Bible commentator Arthur Wallis says:

> Paul used the gift of tongues extensively. . . . Without a doubt praying and giving thanks with the Spirit (i.e., in tongues) played a very important part in the devotional life of this great apostle. Far from disparaging it, as some do, Paul gave thanks to God for the extensive use he was able to make of it.
>
> ... The Holy Spirit is able to illuminate our minds when we are praying over some matter with inadequate knowledge. But there are times when we do not need to know the facts—when perhaps it's important that we *not* know. It is here that praying with the spirit may take over from praying with the mind, enabling us to pray beyond our knowledge of the situation, because the Holy Spirit who inspires the language knows all the facts.
>
> We usually know at such times that our words are intercession, rather than praise or thanksgiving, and although we do not know what we are saying, it is enough to know that the Holy Spirit is inspiring it, and that the prayer will therefore be right "on target." What does it matter that we do not understand the words when we know that God does?[2]

When we yield to the Holy Spirit and take time to listen to his directions, we can pray more effectively in a variety of ways.

Overcoming Intellectual Hang-Ups

Ralph, a thirty-three-year-old Air Force major, went with his wife Tommi on a trip to Israel more than twenty years ago. During the first four days of the tour everyone seemed to be enjoying themselves, seeing the sights of the Holy Land. Everyone, that is, except Ralph. He certainly wasn't having fun, and he knew it was a spiritual problem.

On the fifth night, in a hotel on the Mount of Olives in Jerusalem, he and Tommi were talking late after dinner. "I don't understand why our God is supposedly better than the god worshipped by people who embrace other religions," he said.

"Put your question on hold and I'll be right back," Tommi answered. Then she went to a nearby room to get a couple they had been hanging out with on the tour.

Though it was midnight, these new friends came to Tommi and Ralph's room and began explaining to him God's greatest gift, his Son, who came to earth to die for Ralph's sins and was resurrected from the grave. They explained Jesus had prepared a place in heaven for him—and for all who would believe—but that salvation was possible only through the one true God. For two hours, they opened their Bible and showed Ralph truths from the very words of Jesus.

In the early morning hours, Ralph got on his knees and surrendered his heart to the Lord. "I knew I was saved," he recalls. Two nights later he was with the tour group in a prayer meeting, with all thirty of them holding hands, praying for peace in Israel and for God's glory to pour down. Suddenly Ralph began speaking in tongues—an experience his wife had explained to him several times before.

"It was only two days before that I had come to a full knowledge of salvation," Ralph said. "Now, here I was speaking in tongues and experiencing the presence of the Holy Spirit—it was an intense but exhilarating moment."

What has speaking in tongues meant for this now-retired Air Force colonel?

"It has given me an easy and natural way to pray," he said.

"Especially when I don't know how to pray with my intellect in a given situation. Sometimes when I'm jogging I pray in tongues and in English, too. Looking back, I think it was my intellect that kept me from accepting the Lord sooner." Now, as an elder in one of the largest churches in his state, Ralph unashamedly shares his faith with others, and he has a great sense of freedom about praying in tongues.

Soon after I (Quin) had interviewed Ralph to write this story, a young woman on the West Coast who received the baptism in the Holy Spirit just a year ago called me. "My husband wants what I have—but it's this tongues thing that he's afraid of," she said. "He's an engineer—very intellectual—and he's never heard a man speak in tongues. But I don't know anyone to introduce him to who can help him with this."

How I wished that Ralph could get on a plane and fly to my friend's home to share how God had transformed his prayer life through the gift of tongues. God will have to reach her husband another way. However, I told her the main thing needed was for him to give to God the fear that prevented him from receiving all the gifts God wants to give him.

Receiving God's Abundance

How ironic that believers so often neglect—whether through ignorance, carelessness, pride, or stubbornness—to avail themselves of the help of the Holy Spirit. They may have just enough spiritual food to survive, but they have no abundance of love, joy, peace, power, or provision in their lives. Others may have had an encounter with the Holy Spirit but for various reasons failed to keep walking in a deeper revelation of the experience.

Our friend Kerry was reared in a Christian home and

educated at several different Christian colleges. Once, while a student—more out of curiosity than spiritual hunger—she allowed an evangelist to pray for her to receive the Holy Spirit. Nothing spectacular happened then, but two days later, while lying in bed, praying, she suddenly realized that she was no longer praying in English, but in tongues.

"I prayed like that for three hours, and I never felt better in my life," Kerry said. "But I had no teaching on the Holy Spirit, and I didn't truly understand what had happened to me. I didn't know I could speak in tongues at will, and so for the next eighteen years I never used my prayer language."

Kerry's attitude was like that of people who say, "If God wants me to speak in tongues he'll have to do it to me or through me—I'm not going to initiate it."

Years later, at a church camp, a counselor asked her, "Do you speak in tongues?" Kerry related the experience she'd had in college. "But when you speak in tongues, you're still in control," the counselor explained. "So you can pray in tongues whenever you want to." As they prayed together Kerry began speaking in tongues in several different dialects, and the counselor encouraged her to pray like that several times a day.

"After I began doing what the counselor challenged me to do, my discernment was markedly sharpened," Kerry reports. "The Holy Spirit reveals things to me about those I'm counseling or praying for. Praying in tongues enables me to intercede for others when I have no natural knowledge of what is going on in their lives. Of course I know the Holy Spirit was with me from the time I received Christ, but this deeper experience has been a wonderful gift in my life."

The Hang-Up of "Feeling Worthy"

Numbers of people who have prayed without success to receive the Holy Spirit feel that the failure is because they don't measure up to some elusive standard of holiness. They simply feel they aren't worthy to receive this gift. The reality is, no one actually "deserves" to receive any of God's gifts. He requires only that we become willing to walk in his ways, willing to receive the Holy Spirit he has promised with no strings attached. Through that act of submission, we put ourselves in a position to be empowered by the Holy Spirit to live a more fruitful life than we ever could in our own strength.

Gordon Lindsay provides this valuable insight:

We must get the matter straight. Many people suppose that holiness is conformity to a set of standards arbitrarily set up by men. One may outwardly conform to these things and still have sin in his heart. He may have pride, self-will and self-righteousness.

The fact is, one doesn't receive the Holy Spirit because he has great spiritual attainments, nor because he has developed a strong Christian character. To tell a person he must come up to a certain standard before he can receive may shut him off from the very source by which he can live a victorious life. . . . We need the Holy Spirit in order to bear the fruit of the Spirit.[3]

Well-known author Catherine Marshall, who received the Holy Spirit in the early days of the charismatic renewal, influenced many seekers through her writing. In her book *The Helper* she told how her experience with the Holy Spirit gradually changed her from the inside out. After asking God for this gift, she began to be aware of the Spirit's still, small voice in her heart. When she was about to speak harsh or negative words to someone—or even too many words—she would feel a sharp check on the inside. The Holy Spirit began helping her with daily decisions, and in her witnessing to others of Jesus. She wrote:

> I soon realized that the baptism of the Holy Spirit was no one-time experience, rather a process that would continue throughout my lifetime. True, there was that initial infilling. But how well I knew that I had not thereby been elevated to instant sainthood. In my humanness, self kept creeping back in, so I needed repeated fillings if I were ever to become the mature person God meant me to be.[4]

A Family Is Transformed

Betty, an attractive Canadian homemaker, seemingly had everything a woman could wish for. She had married her college sweetheart, both of them were Christians, he had a successful sales job in aeronautics that took him all over the world, they had three beautiful children. Then a dark blanket of depression settled over Betty's life, leaving her barely able to function or care for her family. Her faith in God caused her to reach out to him for help, and she began reading the Book of Acts to find answers.

"As I read about the miracles which took place in the early church, my mind struggled with the teaching I had heard all my life—that those miracles were only for biblical times," Betty said. "In my church, it never crossed our minds that we could believe God for miracles today. But as I read the Scripture, faith stirred in my heart to pray for deliverance from depression. Alone at home one day I cried out to God for help. Then I commanded the devil to get out of my life, and declared that I was set free in Jesus' name."

Immediately the cloud of depression lifted. Betty called her husband, Willard, to tell him the good news.

"The minute I heard her voice over my office phone, I realized something had changed," Willard said. "Like Betty, I had always been taught that miracles weren't for today, but I knew this definitely was a miracle."

About this time, a husband-and-wife musical team visited their church, and Betty and Willard invited the couple to their home for dinner. They came, along with some other couples in the church who had received the Holy Spirit. Betty's miraculous deliverance from depression had launched her and Willard on a quest for "something more" in their relationship with the Lord. Soon they were participating in a house Bible study group and asking God to fill them with the Holy Spirit.

"I received the Holy Spirit while praying alone in my bedroom," Betty told us. "Suddenly I felt overwhelmed by God's presence and power—it was so strong I felt as if I were going to explode. I began weeping, but for joy, not because I felt sad. After that, I sensed an incredible love for people that I had never experienced before. A short time later when a friend prayed for me to receive my prayer language, I began praising God in another tongue. It was wonderful to use this gift to express my feelings to the Lord. Within those few weeks of time, my life was totally transformed. Later I went through a very painful time of rejection and persecution by other Christians, but the Holy Spirit sustained me and gave me the wisdom to deal with it."

Willard knew his wife's experience was genuine, and he was hungry to draw closer to the Lord, but he struggled with the idea of speaking in tongues.

"My intellect just got in the way, and it held me back," he said. "But finally I prayed, 'God, I want everything you have for me, and if that includes speaking in tongues, then I'm willing.' About that time we attended a conference together. When the leader encouraged everyone to begin worshipping the Lord in tongues, a thunderous sound of praise erupted from the crowd. I said, 'Lord, I'm going to make a noise for you!' As I began shouting praises to him, the next thing I knew I was speaking in tongues, and it was never a problem after that."

After having their lives radically changed by the power of the Holy Spirit, Betty and Willard wanted to help others who needed God's touch on their lives. They sold their home in the suburbs and moved their family to a big house in the inner city. There they began reaching out to street people and drug addicts—people the conventional church was not reaching. Ultimately, Willard left his successful career and he and Betty established a Christian television network in Canada.

"People were so hungry to learn more about the Holy Spirit and the truth of God's Word, and many, like us, weren't receiving the whole truth in their churches," Willard told us. "We felt that God wanted us to help provide them with spiritual food during the entire week through Christian television."

Today, twenty-five years later, one of their sons works alongside them in the growing TV network, and their other two adult children are serving the Lord. When we (Quin and Ruthanne) went to Winnipeg to appear on their TV program, Betty and Willard shared their story with us to include in this book. Truly, theirs is a family that has been transformed by the Holy Spirit.

Beware the Pitfalls

These stories clearly illustrate some common obstacles a diligent seeker must overcome in order to receive the baptism of the Holy Spirit. They include the following:

1. Unbelief—thinking that this experience is not for today (others have persuaded you the gifts died off with the early church), or listening to the enemy's voice in your mind telling you the experience is based on emotionalism, or that speaking in tongues is simply gibberish.
2. Intellectualism—a reluctance to speak in tongues because "it doesn't make logical sense."
3. Fear—not trusting God and believing his gifts are good ones. Some people hesitate to ask, for fear they will be deceived. Jesus said, "If you then, being evil, know how to give good gifts to your children, how much more will your heavenly Father give the Holy Spirit to those who ask Him!" (Lk 11:13, NKJV).
4. A sense of unworthiness—a feeling that you do not deserve this gift. This causes many born-again believers to hold back from asking the Lord to fill them with the Holy Spirit.
5. False expectations—being disappointed when your own spiritual encounter doesn't measure up to what you expected.
6. Stopping your praying in tongues because you don't see the need. (Remember, Fran was interceding for the president of Egypt, although she didn't realize it until later. She also ministered to someone when she prayed in a language the woman could understand, though Fran herself could not.)
7. Not giving the Holy Spirit permission to change your heart and life. (When Betty and Willard sold their home to move to the inner city so they could minister to drug addicts, they

listened to God's directive).

8. Lack of studying the Word and growing in the things of God. (Some people may feel so spiritual that they forget they need to read the Bible daily. This is a necessary step to continuous growth.)

9. Unpleasant results when you impulsively share your experience with everyone you meet, instead of first asking God for guidance. (Face it, some friends may think you're crazy. It's important to pray about *when* and *how* to share with the people who are open and ready to hear.)

10. Criticism or persecution. This is something I (Quin) never expected. I was the most shocked by criticism from friends and spiritual leaders in my own denominational church. When I called the pastor who had prayed for me to receive the Holy Spirit, he was kind but direct. "God never promised us a rose garden," he said. "With the fragrant rose comes the thorns."

We must never deny the power of the Holy Spirit in our lives. He wants us to be willing to be used by him to pray for others, or to share the truth of the Holy Spirit when he prompts us. He is faithful to lead us as we remain open to hearing and obeying his voice.

Prayer

Lord, help me to put aside all the negative thoughts in my mind that prevent me from receiving your truth. I truly want to get beyond the hindrances and hang-ups so that I can receive the Holy Spirit and experience a deeper walk with you. Thank you for drawing me into your presence. Amen.

SIX

How Can I Walk in the Spirit?

If we live in the Spirit, let us also walk in the Spirit.

GALATIANS 5:25, NKJV

To "walk in the Spirit" means to live in moment-by-moment reliance upon the inner guidance of the Holy Spirit. The Greek word for *walk* here literally means "to walk in line with." It is "an exhortation to keep step with one another in submission of heart to the Holy Spirit, and therefore of keeping step with Christ," writes W.E. Vine.[1]

How can we learn to recognize the Spirit's prompting as we seek to follow the Lord? What disciplines clear the way for the Spirit to work? Pastor David Wilkerson of Times Square Church in New York City has expressed it well:

Walking in the Spirit means incredible, detailed direction and unclouded decisions. The Holy Spirit provides absolute, clearly detailed instructions to those who walk in Him. If you walk in the Spirit, then you don't walk in confusion—your decisions aren't clouded ones.

The early Christians did not walk in confusion. They were led by the Spirit in every decision, every move, every action! The Spirit talked to them, and directed them in their every waking hour. No decision was made without consulting Him. The church's motto throughout the New Testament was: "He who has ears to hear, let him hear what the Spirit has to say."[2]

Learning to Listen and Obey

Shortly after the deadly terrorist attacks on the World Trade Center in New York, a friend in Singapore sent me (Ruthanne) a message that clearly illustrates the importance of being led by the Holy Spirit.

This man's sister—we'll call her Heather—was getting ready to go to her job in lower Manhattan on that September 11 Tuesday morning when she felt that the Holy Spirit spoke and told her, "Don't go." She shrugged off the idea, reasoning that since she'd missed work on Monday because of a dental appointment, she really shouldn't miss again. She went ahead and got ready for a day at the office.

Although the prompting was still strong when she reached the subway station, she went ahead and boarded the train. Yet the feeling that she should not go to work became so intense that she got off at the third stop. While she was waiting to take a train back home, all service was suspended. Heather walked upstairs to street level and could see in the distance—in the direction she had been traveling—the north tower collapsing. The street was in total chaos, with people running, many of them crying. Through the smoke and ash-laden streets, she found her way back home, walking for about forty-five minutes to get there.

During her trek home, Heather suddenly remembered that several weeks earlier her pastor, David Wilkerson, had called the congregation at Times Square Church to prayer and fasting. He and the other pastors felt that the Holy Spirit had revealed to them that some kind of turmoil was coming upon the United States. God's people were to fast and pray so that they would be able to stand in the midst of the turmoil. Then she realized that in the midst of the horrible chaos all around her, she felt no panic, only God's peace—and gratitude that the Holy Spirit had kept speaking until she obeyed.

Most of us, like Heather, have sometimes felt a prompting from the Holy Spirit about a particular circumstance. Yet often, because of a sense of duty or perhaps our human reasoning, we tend to ignore the urge and go ahead with our plans. He is faithful to keep speaking to us, but it's important—sometimes a matter of life and death—for us to learn to listen and then obey his leading.

Being Guided by Inner Peace

Sometimes fear is the hindrance that prevents us from sensing the Holy Spirit's clear guidance in a situation. Shortly after the events of September 11, 2001, changed our lives in so many ways, I (Ruthanne) was scheduled to go with my husband to Kiev, Ukraine, to teach at a pastors' conference. In fact, we had already purchased our airline tickets. Yet suddenly everyone was newly aware of the dangers of air travel, as airports went to a heightened state of alert and enacted increased security measures.

Several friends suggested, some insistently, that we should cancel the trip. The scary realities we heard in daily news reports, as well as the genuine concern of our friends and family members, left us feeling confused about what to do. Then I thought of Paul's admonition to Timothy: "For God has not given us a spirit of fear, but of power and of love and of a sound mind" (2 Tm 1:7, NKJV). I knew the final decision shouldn't be based on a fear of flying, or the fear of getting stranded somewhere en route because of unsafe conditions.

John and I prayed specifically for the Holy Spirit's clear direction in the matter, and soon we both felt strongly that we should go ahead with the trip. I sometimes call it being guided by your sense of inner peace. We felt no peace at the prospect of disappointing our Ukrainian friends who had spent months planning this event. Then, as we recalled the ways God had helped us on many previous mission trips in less-than-ideal conditions, we felt confident that his protection and presence would be with us in this situation, too.

We were greatly blessed at the conference, which drew church workers from several cities in the Ukraine. Their enthusiastic response to our teaching was most gratifying. Furthermore, we learned that our presence was especially important because two other speakers scheduled to come from Asia had to cancel because they could not obtain visas.

This confirmed to us the importance of rejecting fear—or a solution based on logic—and depending on the Holy Spirit to guide us. He is faithful and creative in providing the direction we seek when we are sensitive to his signals.

Seizing an Opportunity

Staying alert and open to the Holy Spirit's direction in everyday situations, even while on the job, often provides unexpected opportunities. Dawn is a Spirit-filled nurse who looks for ways to quietly share her faith with her patients. One night, Trina, a pregnant woman struggling with bouts of vomiting and dehydration, checked into the hospital in an attempt to avoid miscarrying her third child. Dawn was assigned to help her get settled in the room and begin treatments.

In unpacking Trina's suitcase, Dawn pulled out a paperback version of the Bible called *The Book* and put it on the bedside table. "That's my favorite book, too," she said with a smile.

"It used to be my favorite," Trina answered glumly.

"Well, maybe God's giving you some time to spend with him while you're in here for rest and recuperation," Dawn responded.

"Yeah, maybe," Trina said, looking out the window.

"Can I pray for you?" Dawn asked, after checking her vital signs and filling in her chart.

"OK," Trina agreed, showing no enthusiasm.

Dawn prayed for healing for the mother and the baby—especially that Trina would have strength to carry it to full term. "Lord, make yourself known to Trina in a powerful way during these next few days," she finished.

After that brief encounter, Dawn's nursing shift changed, and patient and nurse didn't see each other again.

Six years later, Trina attended a women's conference where Quin was teaching. Dawn was there to be Quin's prayer partner, and led a worship chorus to open the session.

Afterward Trina rushed up to Dawn. "I recognized your voice when you began to sing today!" she said. "You're the nurse who prayed for me to carry my baby to full term. That was six years ago, and today we have a healthy, beautiful daughter."

Dawn stared at her. "What about you? You must have had a change of heart to be attending this Christian women's conference."

"After you prayed with me and left the room that night in the hospital, I rededicated my life to the Lord," Trina said. "I confessed that I'd made a big mess of my life, and asked God to help me clean it up. After getting home from the hospital I received the Holy Spirit and tried to live a godly life before my husband, Rick. He was a professional musician, playing rock-and-roll music in bars and clubs. Before this I had been praying, 'Lord, change him.' But after that night in the hospital I prayed, 'Lord, change me,' as I begged God for my husband's salvation. Then Rick agreed to go to church with me one Sunday night."

Later, when one of the men at church responded to Rick's questions about serving the Lord, he committed his musical abilities and his life to Christ. Now he helps with the music and youth ministries at their church, and has become a full-time associate pastor.

"God worked powerfully in my life and my husband's life after you prayed with me in the hospital that day," Trina told Dawn. "Now we have a vision for building a facility to help young women in crisis situations, and God has already provided the land for the project."

We never know what seeds we are planting when we obey the nudges of the Holy Spirit, and most of the time we don't know the result. What a blessing when he occasionally gives us a glimpse, as he did for Dawn in this case, to encourage us to continue obeying his voice as we walk in the Spirit.

A.B. Simpson wrote:

If we would walk in the Spirit we must obey Him when He does speak.... If we will be still and suppress our own impulses and clamorous desires, and will meet Him with a heart surrendered to His will and guidance, we shall know His way (see Psalm 25:9).

... Let us be sensitive to His touch, responsive to His whisper, obedient to His commandments, and able ever to say, "The Father hath not left me alone; for I do always those things that please Him" (John 8:29).[3]

Renewed Faith, Greater Zeal

Colm, a young man who attends my (Quin's) church in Colorado, told me of his experience of receiving the Holy Spirit when he was barely fifteen years old. After being in one historic denomination for several generations, his family began attending a church where the charismatic gifts were accepted and practiced.

One night after attending a class on the baptism of the Holy Spirit, he asked several leaders in the church to pray for him to receive the Holy Spirit. For Colm it was a holy moment, as unspeakable joy flooded through him and he spoke with tongues. However, within six months he allowed peer pressure to diminish his walk with God. As he grew older he drifted from the Lord and into the drug and alcohol scene, yet he never completely lost interest in God and the reality of the Holy Spirit.

"My partying friends always said I'd make a good pastor," he remembers. "Although I was serving as altar boy and janitor at our church, and attending Sunday services, I was not living for God during the week. I knew my relationship with him was not complete, yet I always had a sense of God's presence—like a pulling or nudging from him."

In his third year of college Colm went to Edinburgh, Scotland, for a year of study. Finding himself alone, a student in a foreign land with no friends and no family support system, he grew slightly depressed. When he learned a local church was inviting students to a free dinner, followed by a worship service, he decided to attend. That evening he recommitted his life to the Lord, and the Holy Spirit once again became a strong reality for him.

Now twenty-one years old with a renewed zeal for God, Colm returned to the States to finish his bachelor of arts degree.

Then he went to Colorado to serve in a church internship, helping to develop a youth program while working as a carpenter. "My heart soon turned to evangelism and outreach," he said. "I was determined never to stray from God's will for me again."

On September 11, 2001, Colm was visiting his parents in New York City when the terrorist attack occurred. His dad, whose job was only three blocks from the World Trade Center, had not yet arrived there when the attack came. He headed back to Brooklyn and met Colm at a neighborhood restaurant, then they walked to a nearby hospital to donate blood. Next they headed for their church, across the street from the hospital, where a vestryman had just arrived to open the doors to the sanctuary. Immediately the three of them began praying with the dozens of passersby who came in for prayer, encouragement, and hope.

"I felt the Holy Spirit showing me how to pray for each one who came to me," Colm said. "Some were crying, some couldn't speak English, some were just overwhelmed with grief. I felt I was in my element—my life's calling—to pray for each person individually and tell them of a loving heavenly Father."

Two nights later, armed with his union credentials, he showed up at Ground Zero, donned a hard hat, and began to help remove rubble. "I hurt for this city where I grew up," he told me after he returned home. "The World Trade Center was a special identifying landmark for me—my dad used to take me there to watch fireworks on the Fourth of July. Now I mourn the loss of those who perished and I pray for the people of New York."

Today Colm is confident that the Holy Spirit led him to travel to New York that particular week, and steered and strengthened him throughout the whole experience. He is trusting the Holy Spirit to one day lead him into full-time evangelism ministry.

Sometimes, like Colm, we are led by the Holy Spirit and aren't even aware of it at the time. Think about times in your life when you've had that experience. You are going about your daily life—which at times seems so humdrum—trying to be faithful in your daily disciplines. Then, bang! God moves supernaturally, or gives you an unexpected "divine appointment." Suddenly you realize God has accomplished something extraordinary because you have obeyed his leading.

The Blessing of Obedience

When Anne first received the Holy Spirit, she asked the Lord to speak to her and lead her to reach others. After that she occasionally would feel prompted to do or say something that seemed to be an idea from outside her own thoughts.

"I learned to recognize these times as the Holy Spirit leading me, and I began taking the risk of stepping out in obedience to these leadings," Anne said. "Once, when I was driving down the highway and felt prompted to exit and go into the post office, I obeyed, figuring I had nothing to lose. As I stepped into the post office, praying quietly and listening for God, I saw a woman talking on the pay phone and felt the Lord say to me, 'Go pray for her.' So I walked in her direction, praying as I went, and then I heard, 'Lay hands on her and pray.'"

At that moment Anne had to make a decision. Choosing to obey the prompting, she gently put her hands on the woman's shoulders and continued praying.

"Then I realized that this woman was having a conversation about the Lord," Anne reported. "After a few minutes she hung up the phone and turned around with a tear-streaked face. She told me she had been at home watching a Christian television program that invited people to call for prayer. She didn't even have a telephone in her home, but she was so desperate for God that she decided to go to the post office to use a pay phone to call the prayer line.

"I explained how the Holy Spirit had told me to pull off the highway, go into the post office, and pray for the lady talking on the phone, and she began crying again. The Holy Spirit used me as a tangible sign to this woman to show her that God loves her so much he sent someone just to pray for her."

When the woman asked how she could learn to hear the Lord's voice like that, Anne shared with her about receiving the Holy Spirit and allowing his gifts to operate in your life.

"She wanted the Holy Spirit, so we prayed once again," Anne said. "She left the post office that day full of joy and filled with the power of the Holy Spirit. I left the place filled with the awesome wonder of God and a true lesson on what it means to be led by the Spirit."

Sometimes when you have prayed for something—for example, asking God to change your tendency to worry to an attitude of simple trust—it may take a crisis to make you realize that he has indeed given what you asked for. That's why it is good to daily ask the Holy Spirit to guide your thoughts and actions. The Scripture says, "The steps of a good man are ordered by the Lord, and He delights in his way" (Ps 37:23, NKJV).

The Holy Spirit Provides Strength and Courage in Crisis

In times of crisis we can find ourselves relying both on the Holy Spirit's voice to us and on the Scriptures we have tucked away in our heart. Such was the case with Cheryl.

While she stood in line to make a deposit in a bank in

Ottawa, Ontario, her husband, Andrew, and baby son waited in the car for her. She wouldn't be long because the bank was to close soon. It was ten minutes to eight on a Friday night. As Cheryl stood there, however, a terrible spirit of uneasiness suddenly gripped her. *What is it? What is wrong?* she wondered, as she began praying quietly in tongues.

Then she knew. Two men who had suddenly burst into the bank began making a big commotion, with cursing and threats. "Don't turn around or I'll kill you," one of them said to her. "I have a knife at your back."

The two men were obviously high on drugs and swore loudly. They wore baseball caps and colored bandannas over their mouths to conceal their identities. One waved a gun over the bank customers.

Cheryl tells more about her experience:

I thought about slipping my rings off and placing them in my pocket so the robbers wouldn't take them. As I prayed in tongues under my breath, the Lord began to speak to me.

"Don't do that. Just be still." A sense of God's peace fell over me.

Then the same quiet voice instructed me, *"I am your shield."* A passage popped into my mind. "In Him will I trust ... he is my shield ... my high tower, and my refuge ... my savior; thou savest me from violence. I will call on the Lord, who is worthy to be praised: so shall I be saved from mine enemies" (2 Sm 22:3-4, KJV).

Women around me were crying, some with great sobs. Yet I felt encased in a box of calm and I continued praying in tongues under my breath. The man with the gun suddenly leaped over the counter to scoop money from one cashier's drawer. As he jumped, his bandanna fell off his face, making it easy to identify him. He quickly moved to the next cashier's drawer, then the next one.

Now I thought for sure that we—the witnesses to this crime—might be harmed. We knew what one of the robbers looked like. But the men were so bent on getting as much money as they could, they kept on gathering up the cash. When they finished they ran from the bank, still waving the gun and a knife.

From his vantage point in our car, my husband saw the men when they approached the getaway car. One climbed into the car's trunk, the other jumped in on the passenger side. Then the waiting driver sped toward the freeway to be lost in the heavy weekend traffic.

Miraculously, all of us escaped unhurt. I returned to the car and calmly told my husband how God's peace had surrounded me the whole time. While in the bank, I never stopped praying in tongues. Truly, God was my shield, my high tower, and my refuge. He saved us all from violence that day.

Two months later the robbers were caught because the bank's camera had snapped a photo of the man who lost his mask as he jumped across the counter.[4]

Of course, every tough situation we face has a different set of circumstances, but when we rely on the Holy Spirit to help guide us through crises and hard times, we receive the needed direction, strength, and comfort. He's with us in the scary times as well as in the happier ones.

One of our friends who is a nurse and has experienced a lot of family challenges sometimes laughingly says, "My life seems always to be full of drama and trauma!" Yet, she is one who wholly depends on the Holy Spirit, because she says she really needs his help!

A Holy Spirit Bonus

One of the bonuses I (Quin) noticed about my own devotional time after I received the baptism of the Holy Spirit was that I could understand the Bible more clearly, even certain passages that had bewildered me before. Now, however, I had a new hunger to search out and discover the meaning of so-called obscure verses.

Have you ever been reading the Bible and thought all those genealogies seemed boring? Then a verse would just jump out at you. Such a verse caught my attention years ago. Later it was made popular to millions through a little book called *The Prayer of Jabez* (by Bruce Wilkenson), based on 1 Chronicles 4:10 (NKJV):

> And Jabez called on the God of Israel saying,
> "Oh, that You would bless me indeed,
> And enlarge my territory,
> That Your hand would be with me,
> And that You would keep me from evil,
> That I may not cause pain."

I researched the expression "to bless" and discovered that it means to ask God to impart supernatural favor. So I began praying the prayer of Jabez, asking God to give me supernatural favor and to "enlarge my territory." In other words, I wanted God to give me opportunities to be used by him in a larger sphere of influence. Yet I discovered that it's not always convenient to be available to his plans, even when I've prayed that prayer.

One May morning I was flying from Miami to Atlanta after having been a keynote speaker at a Spanish convention the night before. I'd gotten up at 5:00 A.M. to catch this plane, and all I wanted to do was rest and recuperate from three busy days and nights that had been short on sleep. Before boarding, I'd changed my seat to one closer to the front of the plane. You could say that God had a divine appointment for me that morning—though I wasn't in a frame of mind to desire it.

I soon learned that the woman sitting beside me, Laura, was a career missionary to Argentina. She was coming to the United States to undergo a thorough physical examination and visit family members she hadn't seen for three years. I asked about her work among the Spanish-speaking people where she lived. She began sharing about her ministry, and sleepy as I was, my curiosity was aroused. Sensing a nudge of the Holy Spirit to pay attention to this woman, I laid aside my expectations for a nap.

As we talked, she mentioned that she had read the book *Intercessory Prayer*, written by my pastor, Dutch Sheets. That really grabbed my attention. Then she asked, "Do you have the baptism of the Holy Spirit?"

"Yes," I replied. "I had an experience nearly thirty years ago that dramatically changed my life."

After sharing with her some startling things God has done for me, I opened my Bible to the Book of Acts. For the rest of our flight, I took her on a biblical journey, explaining the outpouring of the Holy Spirit in the early church and bringing it up to date with what I knew of revival since the early 1900s in our country.

Occasionally she'd stop me with such comments as, "If this is a gift from God, he can give it to me anytime he likes, but he hasn't … I've always been taught that speaking in tongues is not for us today … My church doesn't believe we need a second touch from God to live a victorious Christian life ... They said I got all of the Holy Spirit when I first believed in Jesus ... If we believed what you're saying about the Holy Spirit, our mission board wouldn't allow us to stay at our assignment."

Instead of trying to argue with her, I prayed quietly in tongues when silence fell between us. I asked the Holy Spirit to speak to her as she meditated about all we'd discussed. Finally, she posed her final question.

"Do you think I could really receive this gift? Are you sure all I have to do is ask?"

"Of course you can," I said, instructing her how to pray to receive the baptism in the Holy Spirit. I also prayed she would experience the Lord's peace and love and joy as she made this important decision.

The plane landed and we went our separate ways. I've sent her books and recommended various Bible commentaries to her. I may never hear back from her, but I know I obeyed the Holy Spirit that day as I planted seeds of truth. Laura obviously is on an intense spiritual search, and I pray her life will be touched and changed as she receives the fullness of God's Spirit.

My Jabez prayer was answered in an amazing way on that flight. God enlarged my territory and gave me an opportunity to share with a needy person who was hungry for more of him. The Holy Spirit directed my conversation, showed me exactly which Scriptures to share, and led me to pray for her. My own life was enriched by the experience.

I can tell you truthfully, in the days before I had received the baptism in the Holy Spirit, I would have rolled my head toward the window and caught some sleep, ignoring everyone around me. In fact, I wouldn't even have known where to look in the Bible to find answers to her questions.

If we want to walk in the Spirit, we need to learn to recognize his voice with distinct preciseness, and obey his direction. We should be willing to spend whatever time it takes in his presence to reach this level of intimacy with him. Walking in the Spirit is an adventure you won't want to miss!

Can God Really Speak to Me?

God has used our friend Beth Alves to teach hundreds of spiritual warriors the important guidelines on how to hear from God. In her book *The Mighty Warrior* she says:

> Drawing near to the Lord opens the door for Him to fellowship and communicate with you.... The Lord speaks to you through the person of the Holy Spirit (Ezekiel 36:27; John 14:16-17).
> ... One way to know whether you are hearing the Holy Spirit is to use this test: Does the voice gently lead you in a direction, or is it commanding and harsh? God's voice gently guides and encourages, giving you hope (Psalm 18:35; Isaiah 40:11; James 3:17). GOD LEADS, SATAN DRIVES (John 10:4). God convicts, Satan condemns and brings guilt (Psalm 8:1-2). God woos, Satan tugs hard. When God speaks, He does not use fear to motivate. If fear overcomes you, it is the enemy speaking, not God (2 Timothy 1:7).

Beth gives these guidelines to hearing the voice of God:

- Bind the voice of the enemy [that is, command Satan to be silent].
- Submit your own will and reasoning to the Holy Spirit.
- Turn off your own problems.

- Give your undivided attention to God's Word.
- Limit your own talking.
- Write it down. (The Spirit of the Lord will speak to you through impressions or pictures in the theater of your mind. When this happens, write them down.)
- Don't argue mentally.
- Wait upon the Lord for the interpretation.
- Don't get ahead of or lag behind the Holy Spirit.
- The Holy Spirit sometimes speaks through music. Listen.
- Pay attention to your dreams. Write them down. Not all dreams are of God.
- Don't be afraid of silence. Don't be upset if you don't hear anything when you pray. The Holy Spirit may just want you to worship the Lord.[5]

Prayer

Thank you, Lord, for the gift of the Holy Spirit that enables me to walk in victory through every difficulty. Forgive me for the times I've failed to wait for your direction and walked in my own strength. Thank you for your faithfulness in redeeming my mistakes. Lord, help me to tune out the clamor of the world, the flesh, and the devil, and listen for your still, small voice. Speak by your Holy Spirit and direct my path, leading me to the divine appointments of your choosing. I pray that my walk and my words will honor and glorify you, in Jesus' name, Amen.

SEVEN

Renewal That Endures

He saved us through the washing of rebirth and renewal by the Holy Spirit, whom he poured out on us generously through Jesus Christ our Savior.

TITUS 3:5-6

Many who criticize the Holy Spirit movement charge that most people's experience of being renewed by the Holy Spirit is a short-lived emotional "high."

Admittedly, both of us (Quin and Ruthanne) can think of individuals who once had an exciting encounter with the Holy Spirit but who now have grown cold in their walk with God. However, for the overwhelming majority of people we know and have interviewed about the Holy Spirit, their renewal experience has been long term and life changing.

Sometimes God moves in our lives in unexpected ways at unexpected times, just to respond to the love we express to him. That's what happened to nineteen-year-old Mell in our next story.

A Cry for Commitment

Mell was excited to leave his studies behind to head home for the Thanksgiving holidays during his first year in college. He had a lot to be thankful for, because just three months earlier he had become a Christian. During his visit home, he was alone in his room late one night, listening with great interest to a cassette tape recounting the story of missionaries in East Germany.

The person telling the story described how the police had threatened to arrest those who were sharing their faith in Christ with others. Suddenly a three-day-old believer boldly declared to the others in the evangelistic team, "If you're afraid, you can go back, but I'm going to march on for Jesus."

"Those words cut through me like a knife," Mell said. "I began to weep and pray, 'Lord, I've known you for three months, but I don't know whether I'd be willing to go to jail for you. Here is a three-day-old believer who is willing to die for you!' I quickly slid out of my chair, fell to my knees, and in desperation started crying out for God to help me become as committed as that new Christian was.

"While I was surrendering my life completely to Christ's Lordship, I began to worship him in a deeper way than I'd ever done before. For the first time, my hands instinctively stretched out to him in loving adoration as I sensed his presence in the room. I had never felt so close to my heavenly Father. Then, as I praised him aloud, I began expressing the deepest longings of my spirit in another language. I had heard of this experience before, but nobody had prayed for me to receive the baptism in the Holy Spirit. In this holy moment it was simply me and the Lord."

Obviously shocked and bewildered by what had just happened, Mell opened his Bible to search for answers and felt led to read through the Book of Acts for the first time. Without any preconceived theological ideas to hinder him, he concluded that the Bible teaches this experience as typical for New Testament believers.

"I've never doubted the authenticity of what I experienced

that autumn night twenty-eight years ago," he said.

After completing his training, Mell went on to serve for several years as a missionary in Guatemala. Now he serves as director of church relations for the National Association of Local Church Prayer Leaders, a network encouraging and empowering prayer in churches throughout the United States.

Renewal and Restoration

Beverly is a friend who discovered the renewing power of the Holy Spirit in the midst of her desperation. Though she had been a faithful Christian during childhood and her teens, her college activities crowded God out of her life, especially after she met Tom. Two years later they were married in a church wedding, but they never made room for the Lord in their relationship.

"During those years I still believed in God," Beverly said, "but I had drifted away from him. Soon things began to go wrong with our perfect marriage—though outwardly we were attractive, young, and successful. My husband, having given up on God because of traumas during his childhood, was full of repressed anger. I reacted by withdrawing from him and shutting down.

"When our first son was born we joined a church, but we were merely going through the motions. I had a good job and the respect of my coworkers, but I was miserable. By the time our second son was born four years later, I was in a state of chronic depression, began drinking heavily, and suffered with migraine headaches. I wouldn't open the curtains or venture outside unless I had to, and I almost never answered the telephone or the doorbell. Despite having two perfect children, I couldn't shake my depression."

Meanwhile, Tom began having fits of rage, after which he wouldn't speak to Beverly for days. As he heaped blame upon her for their problems, she became more depressed and he became suicidal. They were church members during this time, and Tom was in a leadership position, yet their lives only became more miserable.

But within the church was a small group of people who had received the Holy Spirit, and they met regularly for prayer. When they discerned that this young couple had serious problems, they began reaching out to Beverly and Tom. One day when a woman in the group phoned, Beverly was suffering with a migraine and agreed to let her come by the house to pray. After prayer Beverly sensed God's peace, and her headache receded.

Then the lady told her about the baptism of the Holy Spirit. She explained how this would enable her to use a new prayer language to talk to God. She also read from Romans 8:26: "In the same way, the Spirit helps us in our weakness. We do not know what we ought to pray for, but the Spirit himself intercedes for us with groans that words cannot express."

"Amazingly, that was the only Scripture verse I had ever underlined in my Bible as a child," Beverly reported. "Since I always kept my problems to myself, I was delighted with the idea of being able to talk directly to God like that—and I knew I needed to get close to him again. That night I knelt alone beside my bed and silently told God that if he had something more for me, I wanted it. When I opened my mouth to speak, this beautiful language came out. I knew I was talking to God. It seemed his presence enveloped me, and my headache and depression lifted instantly."

That was the beginning of Beverly's complete renewal. A local pastor counseled her and began teaching her truths concerning the Holy Spirit. Two weeks later she found the courage to tell Tom what had happened, only to discover that he had experienced the same thing but had been afraid to tell her. Today, with a restored marriage, they minister to the homeless people in their community through a distribution center that the Lord helped them obtain.

"Our intensive study of God's Word was like massive doses of radiation that healed and restored us, and now we want to help bring hope and restoration to others," Beverly reports. "Of course the enemy has tried to draw me back into depression and sickness—he always tests a victory. But I've found that by regularly staying in the Word and praying in the Spirit, I'm strengthened to stand against these attacks. Also, through the Word and during my prayer times, the Holy Spirit reveals any area in my life that is unpleasing to the Lord."

As we talked to people about their experiences with the Holy Spirit, we were struck by how drastically these encounters changed people's lives—not just temporarily, but for the long term. That is certainly true of Beverly and Tom, as well as the couple in our next story.

Holy Spirit Intercession

Mary and her husband Ken both grew up in a denominational background where they attended church but never experienced the reality of salvation. Of course, they understood nothing about the Holy Spirit. However, after their children were born they began attending a variety of churches, finding a new one wherever Ken's job happened to cause them to settle. Then they ended up in Iowa, where they could not find a good church in their community.

"I was in a state of depression, and my sister-in-law asked if she could pray for me," Mary told us. "She prayed for quite awhile in tongues, then she asked me to say, 'Jesus is Lord.' But when I opened my mouth to speak, I said, 'Satan is lord.' I was totally embarrassed at what had come out of my mouth, because I was an active churchgoer and Bible study leader at the time. (The Lord revealed to me later that when I was a teenager I had played with a Ouija board and a spirit of deception had come on me to cause me to think I was already born again.)

"My sister-in-law rebuked the devil and had me renounce him from every area of my life. When she led me in the prayer of salvation and had me say over and over, 'Jesus is Lord,' I was immediately born again. Then she prayed for me to be baptized in the Holy Spirit, and told me to open my mouth and let the words come out. For months, while in prayer, I kept opening my mouth, but nothing came out. Three months later, when my husband was born again and Spirit-filled, someone told me I actually had to speak the words I was hearing in my mind. I did this, and for about a month I had only a few words. But gradually more words were added to my prayer language.

"Since then the Holy Spirit has sometimes caused us to know beforehand when our children would be in trouble and as we prayed they were protected. Two instances come to mind:

"One night Ken and I were sleeping soundly when both of us awoke at 2:30 A.M. and felt the need to pray. The Lord didn't reveal anything specific to us, but we prayed in the Spirit until the urgency lifted, then went back to sleep. Early the next morning, our daughter, Carla, called for us to come get her at her friend's house, where she had spent the night. When I picked her up she told us that at 2:30 that morning her friend's mother had come home drunk and began attacking her (Carla), throwing things at her and cursing her because we were Christians.

Then suddenly she just stopped and left the room. It was a few hours later when our daughter called us.

"Another time, as I was praying, I had a strong impression that there was 'danger in Paris.' For more than a week I prayed in tongues for this situation during my regular prayer time, although I had no idea what it might mean. Then the burden lifted. Five months later, Carla went to Spain with her high school Spanish class. When she got home from the trip she flew into the house and said, 'Mom, you will never believe what happened to me in Paris!' That was the first time the thought of danger in Paris had crossed my mind since I'd prayed about it months earlier. She told me that while she was waiting at the airport in Paris she noticed the police were watching her. Finally they came over and asked if the suitcase sitting next to her was hers, and she told them, 'No.' The authorities took the suspicious suitcase outside and found a bomb inside! How we praise God for protecting our daughter. I think all parents need this gift of the Holy Spirit to pray effectively for their children."

No Longer Driven by Ambition

One day Marilyn was having lunch with her friend Alice, a volunteer telephone counselor for a local Christian television studio. On this particular day, Alice was feeling discouraged. "With all the calls I took this morning, I didn't have a single opportunity to pray with someone to receive Jesus," she said.

Out of curiosity, Marilyn asked for more details.

Alice handed her a card with a prayer printed on it that she always used while leading someone to pray for salvation.

"I can pray that if you like—I believe it," Marilyn said, after reading the card. So Alice encouraged her to pray aloud.

Marilyn read the prayer aloud and made Jesus her Lord.

"Now you need the baptism of the Holy Spirit," Alice said, handing her another card. "Read this prayer and see if you can agree. You are going to need power to live this Christian life you've just entered."

Again, after looking over the card, Marilyn read the prayer aloud, asking Jesus to baptize her in the Holy Spirit and give her a prayer language. At first, when she spoke only two syllables— Aaa-bbaa (Abba)—she was quite disappointed, and questioned whether she had actually spoken in tongues. Alice reminded her that her first syllables were the Hebrew word for father. This greatly bolstered Marilyn's faith, and within a few months her prayer language became more fluent.

"I was a 'driven woman' before I had this experience," Marilyn said. "I ran at least four miles a day, and was working on a dissertation to finish my doctorate. I also was teaching at a nearby university, besides being mom to four children and wife to a busy professional. But everything changed after I received the Holy Spirit. All I wanted was to pursue God—not education or a prestigious degree."

Soon she dropped out of university and spent more and more of her time attending a Bible study to learn more about the Bible. When the local chapter of a women's charismatic organization in New York was looking for officers, Marilyn was chosen as president. Now she had the opportunity to invite well-known speakers to address the group and share about the power of the Holy Spirit. In this position, Marilyn was able to lead many women to receive Christ and to be filled with the Holy Spirit.

After attending a few meetings with her, Marilyn's husband realized that he, too, needed this experience. Both of them had grown up in a church where they weren't encouraged to read the Bible, so they came into the charismatic experience hungry for spiritual food.

"He always knew that salvation was a gift from God—not something to earn—so it was easier for him to accept what he was now learning from the Bible," Marilyn explained. "We have moved to a different area now, but every week we fill our home with about a hundred young people who come for food, fun, and fellowship. In this setting we make sure they hear about Jesus' love and plan for their lives."

One time when she was praying for the salvation of her son, Marilyn said her prayer language changed to what she calls "warfare tongues."

"I don't know how to explain it, but I know it was intense prayer for his salvation," she said. "I still speak in that tongue when I pray for him."

We don't mean to imply that a person should give up educational pursuits when they receive the Holy Spirit. Yet Marilyn was certain God wanted her to do this, so she obeyed—and she has never regretted it. The Lord has helped her to use her keen mind in explaining spiritual truths to other "intellectuals" in a way they can comprehend.

Praying in the Supernatural Realm

A powerful intercessor we've known for many years first began praying and praising the Lord in tongues during her early childhood, though it was only when she was an adult that she learned the significance of this gift. She shares the story in her own words:

When I was a little girl I would talk to Jesus and then sing in a different language. Mama would say, "JoAnne, I've never heard anyone sing like that. You are in rhythm with something I can't understand." But I'd just tell her I was talking to Jesus. Upon turning twelve, when I was permitted to join the church, my grandfather took me aside after the service, laid hands on my head, blessed me, and then asked the Lord to give me all the gifts of the Holy Spirit.

Years later, when I was in my thirties and the renewal movement was sweeping across America, I attended a lay witness mission. Some of the leaders there prayed for me to receive the baptism of the Holy Spirit, and I received a gusher of words—languages just poured out of me. Then the Lord reminded me that I used to pray like this all the time when I was very small.

Did it make a difference in my life? You bet it did. As my prayers became more forceful I realized that the most powerful thing I could do was to pray in tongues. Praying like this builds me up, cheers me up, fills me up, and fires me up. It enables me to pray beyond my intellect—the thinking realm—and pray in the God realm. It takes me from natural to supernatural praying. God gives me revelations as I pray mysteries to him and he speaks back to me his mysteries. I have prayed in tongues for as long as twelve hours at a time. It brings an anointing on my life, and a closeness to the Lord. It releases the power of God within me. I have traveled to many nations, serving on prayer teams, and when I don't know how to intercede for a given situation, I always rely on praying in the Holy Spirit.

Praying in Tongues Is Effective

Paul wrote, "Anyone who speaks in a tongue should pray that he may interpret what he says. For if I pray in a tongue, my spirit prays, but my mind is unfruitful. So what shall I do? I will pray with my spirit, but I will also pray with my mind." (1 Cor 14:13-15a). He also advised believers to "pray in the Spirit on all occasions with all kinds of prayers and requests" (Eph 6:18a).

"Times of prayer are always dominated by something—our self-pity, our sin, our family needs or need for money, or His Spirit and His kingdom," says Pastor Ted Haggard. "The primary way to turn away from our own interests and become absorbed by His is to pray in the Spirit.... I find that as I pray in tongues, my priorities and thoughts are sharpened. My attitudes change, my inner man is strengthened, my faith is increased, and God drops fresh ideas into my mind."[1]

I (Ruthanne) heard one pastor teach that when we pray in tongues, we should ask God to reveal to us the interpretation of what we have been praying. He gave the example of facing a dilemma when the Christian school that was a part of his church had completely outgrown their facility. The opening of school was only a few weeks away, they had more students enrolled than they had space for, and they had no prospects in sight for acquiring more space in such a short time. As he was worrying about the problem and trying to come up with a solution, he felt the Lord remind him that he should simply pray in the Spirit.

Kneeling on the floor of his office, he began praying in tongues. Then he asked the Lord to reveal the interpretation. Immediately the idea came that he should call a certain businessman whom he knew owned a building not far from the church campus. It was rather late at night, but the pastor called this Christian businessman, told him of his dilemma, and asked whether he would be interested in selling the building. The man was stunned. "Just today I signed an agreement to put that property on the market tomorrow," he said, "but if you're interested, I'll meet you there tonight."

"OK," the pastor said; then he began praying in the Spirit for direction on making an offer. When the two met at the property that night and talked about the possibilities, the pastor felt impressed to make an offer that was far below the actual market value of the building. The owner immediately accepted, and they shook hands on the agreement. The next day, when the news came out that the building was being sold, much larger bids came in from other companies in town. Yet the owner said, "No, I shook hands with the pastor at midnight last night, and I'm selling the property to the church for their Christian school."

The pastor cited several other instances when praying in tongues, then asking for the interpretation, gave him insight into what God's will was for a specific situation. "This is a gift God has given us, but it's been largely neglected," he said. We need to be reminded—as the apostle Paul reminded Timothy—to stir up the gift of God that is in those of us who have been filled with the Holy Spirit (see 2 Tm 1:6).

Often we may pray in tongues and know it's for a particular person, but we may not know the reason. Lyn, who is president of a Christian women's organization in her town, tells of an experience when she knew she was praying for her mom. She tells her story:

On a recent summer night, while driving home, I came close to the exit to turn off to my mom's home when the

Holy Spirit prompted me to pray in tongues fervently, and with a sense of urgency. I started to turn and go to her house, then noticed it was 9:20 P.M. Earlier in the day she'd phoned to say she'd be going to bed by 9:00 P.M. and not to call her after that.

So I continued to pray. I even picked up the phone, once I was home, then put it down before I dialed. Most of the night I prayed. Early the next morning I called to check on her.

She told me of her close escape from tragedy the evening before. In preparing for a ladies' tea to be held in her home the following afternoon, she'd lit two brand-new candles in the dining room so they'd be ready to burn at the tea. But when she went to put the matches back in a bathroom drawer, she forgot to extinguish the candles, and instead went to bed.

The candles burned all night. The next morning when she awoke, flames were starting up the dining room wall. Not only was that wall scorched but the top of the sideboard was burned and the room filled with smoke.

Praise God, the house did not burn down! The room had to be repainted and the top of the sideboard replaced. I believe she was saved because the Holy Spirit prompted me to pray in tongues and God protected her. Her smoke alarm did not go off, and it has since been replaced. Yet nothing can replace the intervention in prayer that comes when we are yielded to the Holy Spirit and we obey that urge to pray in tongues.

Another time, in the middle of February, an intense ice storm with high winds hit our town. Trees were toppled on buildings and in roads. Electricity was out in every home for several days. My mother, a widow who had been alone for a dozen years, had recently remarried. She and her husband were shivering from lack of heat, so I took them a kerosene heater on Saturday night.

At 3:00 A.M. that same night the Lord woke me up to pray. I knew I was praying for them, though I was praying in tongues. Once in a while I'd pray in English—asking for God's protection over them—then go back to praying in tongues. At daybreak I dialed their home. They had just awakened to find that the heater had malfunctioned during the night. Fire had burned the carpet in a small area under the heater, and smoke was filling the house. Yet they were fine.

I believe their lives and their home were spared because the Holy Spirit awakened me to pray for them. How grateful I am for the gift of praying in the Spirit when I don't know how to pray with my intellect, and for the results of that middle-of-the-night prayer.

A Deeper Life of Prayer

One autumn night in 1966 Joan quietly said "yes" to Christ after listening to a Billy Graham crusade sermon on television. "I knew beyond a doubt that I was born again because I'd accepted Jesus," she remembers.

Six months later, hungry for the things of God, she purchased two charismatic books. *They Speak with Other Tongues*, by John Sherrill, answered many of her questions about the biblical validity of speaking in tongues. *The Cross and the Switchblade*, the story of New York street evangelist David Wilkerson, caught her attention because she lived near New York City, the scene of the story. She read how hundreds of gang members and drug addicts became Christians, were baptized in the Holy Spirit, and then began seeing miracles happen in response to prayer. "When a drug addict is instantly delivered and becomes radical for Christ, you know that's a miracle of God," she says.

When the bookstore clerk invited Joan to the Wednesday night service at a nearby Pentecostal church, she responded eagerly.

"The singing was lively, the preaching exalted Christ, and the meeting ended with an invitation for people to be prayed for to receive the baptism of the Holy Spirit," Joan said. "People from all denominations went there regularly. The pastor was wise to insist that those who received the Holy Spirit stay in their own churches and be a light for Jesus there. After I received the baptism of the Holy Spirit, I noticed that while previously my prayer times usually had been short, now I would pray in tongues for long periods of time. I just wanted to talk to God in this beautiful new way of expressing my love and praise to him."

Joan received the Holy Spirit shortly before Easter, but soon noticed that her prayer language changed. "Over Easter week, when I would pray in tongues, I would weep and weep. As this grief kept sweeping over me, I somehow knew that what I felt was the heartache of God the Father over what his Son endured on the cross for my sins.

"In my mind's eye I saw myself some years earlier, kneeling beside my own son after he'd been hit by a car and was still lying in the street. Now I was feeling a grief similar to that of Father God. Someone later explained to me that I was probably interpreting my own prayer language. At the time I didn't know you could interpret what you were praying in tongues."

For a long time before this experience, Joan had tried without success to stop smoking. Yet after receiving the Holy Spirit she lost all desire to smoke. To her it was an immediate sign that Christ indeed was working in her.

When Joan took her pastor's wife with her to one of the Wednesday meetings, she, too, received the Holy Spirit. The pastor was convinced that the experience was real, because his wife was a very intellectual person, not a fanatic. Eventually a group of people from Joan's church who had been baptized in the Spirit began to meet for prayer once a week—a meeting approved by the pastor. Later the charismatic meeting was moved from the church to Joan's house, with the support of her husband, Andy.

For eighteen years, until the death of the pastor, Joan and many of her friends attended the little Pentecostal church for a Bible study on Wednesdays. On Sunday, however, she attended her own church, and she remained involved with the various committees. Today she is still active in the prayer ministry of this church, but her greatest joy is to pray for other women to receive the baptism of the Holy Spirit as she serves as area president for a women's charismatic organization with outreaches into many ethnic groups in the New York City area.

As these stories have shown, God moves by his Spirit in very personal and intimate ways in our lives. Sometimes he speaks to us when we are alone seeking him, and we respond with outstretched arms, as Mell did. At other times he uses other people to share his truths with us, as Marilyn experienced.

The baptism of the Holy Spirit is a gift for you, a believer. It is not reserved only for a few, or just for those whose stories you have read in this book. As you ask for and receive this gift of the Holy Spirit, you will find that your experience can bring a renewal that endures—one that is both life-changing and long-lasting.

Prayer

Father, forgive me for thinking I have to measure up to some standard to receive the gift of the Holy Spirit. Forgive me for judging others because I thought they were merely on an emotional high. Lord, I want renewal in my own life. I am desperate for you. Come and fill me to overflowing with your Spirit. Bring others into my life to help me in my spiritual walk. Thank you, Lord, for answering my prayer. Amen.

EIGHT

The Holy Spirit in History

And afterward, I will pour out my Spirit on all people. Your sons and daughters will prophesy, your old men will dream dreams, your young men will see visions. Even on my servants, both men and women, I will pour out my Spirit in those days.

JOEL 2:28-29

Some eight hundred years after the prophet Joel wrote these words, the apostle Peter stood before a crowd of curious people on the Day of Pentecost in Jerusalem. The people were mystified because they had heard the followers of Jesus speaking in different languages. "This is what was spoken by the prophet Joel" (Acts 2:16), Peter explained as he began his famous sermon—which resulted in some three thousand people accepting Christ that day.

At the close of his message, Peter declared that the gift of the Holy Spirit was given for all believers, not just the apostles and their contemporaries. "The promise is for you and your children and for all who are far off—for all whom the Lord our God will call" (Acts 2:39).

Why the Scarcity of Tongues?

Throughout the history of the church, many theologians have taught that the baptism of the Holy Spirit, with the evidence of speaking in tongues, ceased with the death of the last apostle. However, research by other scholars reveals that this practice never completely died out in the church. It simply became less common because of declining spirituality.

One commentator makes this observation:

> The church's departure from the faith and fervor of Bible days—not a change in God's plan—was the reason for the scarcity of tongues and other gifts from post-apostolic days to the Protestant Reformation. As worldliness crept in and tradition took the place of truth, the gifts and power of God waned and all but disappeared. Scholars of church history admit that the post-apostolic church declined sharply from the spirit and standards of apostolic days.[1]

The authors of an excellent resource, *Speaking in Other Tongues: A Scholarly Defense*, cite dozens of documents that report on various revival movements in which speaking in tongues and other miraculous manifestations occurred. From the time of the early church fathers up to the seventeenth, eighteenth, and nineteenth centuries, such credible accounts exist.

John Wesley (1703-91), the founder of Methodism, had an encounter with the Holy Spirit in May 1738 that changed his life and led to a revival that continued until his death more than fifty years later.[2] In one of his sermons, Wesley wrote:

> There is nothing either in the Old Testament or the New which teaches that miracles were to be confined within the limits of the apostolic or the [post-apostolic] age, or that God hath precluded himself from working miracles of any kind or degree, in any age to the end of time.[3]

Sarah Edwards, wife of the evangelist Jonathan Edwards (1703-58), spoke of a seventeen-day period during the out-pouring of the Spirit in 1740 and 1741 when she experienced love, power, and what she called "the sweet nearness of God." She wrote, "One evening these words, 'The Comforter is come,' were accompanied to my soul with such conscious cer-tainty, and such intense joy, that immediately it took away my strength, and I was falling to the floor, when some of those who were near me caught me and helped me up."[4]

Charles G. Finney (1792-1875), a renowned evangelist of the nineteenth century, came to be known as the "Father of Modern Revivalism." He wrote about receiving "a mighty bap-tism in the Holy Ghost," when he "literally bellowed out the unutterable gushings of my heart."[5]

R.A. Torrey (1856-1928), a noted Congregational minister, once told of a service in London where the American evangel-ist Dwight L. Moody (1839-99) stood up to preach. Instead of preaching his sermon, however, Moody began speaking in another language. "He tried again, with similar results. The third time, after prayer and praise, he was able to preach his mes-sage."[6]

The anointed preaching of Charles H. Spurgeon (1834-92) drew thousands of Londoners to his six-thousand-seat Metropolitan Tabernacle year after year. One British preacher said, "The evangelist once asked his audience to forgive him that when he got especially happy in the Lord, 'I break forth into a kind of gibberish which I do not myself understand.'"[7]

The Birth of the Pentecostal Movement

One can read of numerous revival groups that impacted the history of the church: the Montanists, the Waldensians, Martin Luther's protests which led to the Reformation, the Huguenots, the Moravians, the reformers of the Great Awakening, and so on. Through the years, these movements brought a renewed emphasis on the Holy Spirit, infusing life and growth into the church with speaking in tongues, healings, prophecies, and other miraculous signs. Yet the phenomenon that occurred at the dawn of the twentieth century is the major event that birthed what is now called the Pentecostal movement.

At a Bible school in Topeka, Kansas, the director, Charles Parham, challenged his students to search the Scriptures to see if they could find any reason why they should not receive the Holy Spirit and speak with other tongues. Their studies produced no such proof. On December 31, 1900, the students gathered for a watchnight prayer service to ask for God's blessings to come upon them in the new year. In the early hours of January 1, 1901, a young woman named Agnes Ozman asked the leader to lay hands on her and pray that she might receive the Holy Spirit. When he did so, she began speaking in Chinese, and was unable to speak English for three days.[8]

A few years later, in 1906, William J. Seymour—who had studied under Charles Parham—led a revival at a church on Azusa Street in downtown Los Angeles. For three and a half years, the church conducted services three times a day, seven days a week. In these meetings, thousands of visitors from all over the world received the Holy Spirit and spoke in tongues. In most cases, those who experienced this phenomenon were expelled from their denominational churches and accused of theological heresy. The revival led to the founding of numerous Pentecostal denominations worldwide, and these groups rapidly became the fastest-growing segment of Christianity.

William Booth-Clibborn (teenage grandson of Catherine Booth, founder of the Salvation Army) received the Holy Spirit in London in 1908. Over the next several decades he taught and preached of the experience, in the United States and many other nations of the world. In relating his own testimony of being baptized in the Holy Spirit and speaking in tongues, he wrote:

> The very suggestion that another can take possession of our mouths is an absurdity to the carnal mind. But here was the fact—my natural ability and God's supernatural power could not both manipulate the muscles of speech at the same time. Many saints of God, when reaching this crisis, often asked God to lift His hand, unable to endure such a pressure of supernatural power. They were ignorant of the fact that the *glossalalia* [speaking in other tongues] was the next thing to come.[9]

Within this revival movement, which swept across the world, immature and unwise practices sometimes occurred—which only reinforced the position of the "cessationists" who denied the validity of the baptism of the Holy Spirit. Booth-Clibborn had this to say of such criticism:

> Many times I have listened in amazement at the denunciations of prominent Bible teachers and Christian leaders as they railed against and ridiculed that which has been here

witnessed to. Such unbecoming raging and ranting always left the audience chilled and confused and it has always failed to convince.

... This is a worldwide outpouring of the Spirit of God, a mighty life-giving river of refreshing waters. We should not condemn the whole sweeping tide of waters because at its side we happen to discover a few eddies filled with debris, driftwood and dead fish. Granted that a few stagnant pools may be found where the current has subsided or altered its course; still the main stream flows on full of power and blessings. . . . All supposed refutations and elaborate exposés only excite renewed investigation. The sincere heart, persevering to receive God's best, will not be deceived by all the ecclesiastical clamor.[10]

The Influence of Women

A major distinction of the Pentecostal revival was the influence of women evangelists, the most famous of which were Aimee Semple McPherson (1890-1944) and Maria Woodworth-Etter (1844-1924), who had a profound influence on the Garlock family. Edmund Garlock (Ruthanne's grandfather-in-law) was a hopeless alcoholic and drug addict whose violent temper caused much grief for his wife, Jessie, and twelve children.

When Jessie heard that Mrs. Woodworth-Etter was conducting a tent revival in the area, she bought a train ticket to Long Hill, Connecticut, and gave it to Edmund. "I want you to go to that meeting and stay until God does something for you," she told him. "Don't come back home until you're changed." He did as she requested. A few days later he returned, gathered Jessie and the children around him, and told them he had been saved, healed, delivered, and filled with the Holy Spirit. Life in the Garlock household changed dramatically as the following months proved his conversion to be real. Soon, every member of the family had been filled with the Holy Spirit. Many of the children, including the eldest, H.B. Garlock (Ruthanne's father-in-law), entered full-time ministry.

A New Wave of Renewal

From the early 1900s to the 1950s, the baptism of the Holy Spirit with speaking in other tongues was experienced almost exclusively within Pentecostal groups. Then, by ones, twos, and threes, various denominational pastors began receiving the Holy Spirit. In California in November 1959, Episcopal priest Dennis Bennett told his congregation that he had received the Holy Spirit and spoken in other tongues. He resigned under pressure and accepted the pastorate of St. Luke's parish in Seattle, a church on the verge of being closed.

About this time, when *Time* and *Newsweek* magazines published stories of his experience, the publicity seemed to generate the sense of "a new movement of the Spirit."[11] Attendance at Father Bennett's church more than quadrupled, drawing people from all denominations who were hungry for the Holy Spirit. His lectures and his book about receiving the Holy Spirit, *Nine O'Clock in the Morning*, had widespread influence among liturgical churches across the United States.

By the 1960s the Holy Spirit had "jumped the fence," so to speak, as denominational Christians, Protestant and Catholic, clergy and laymen, began receiving the Holy Spirit and speaking in tongues in huge numbers. Pope John XXIII, at the Vatican II Council (1962-65), expressed his desire for a new

Pentecost and directed the churches to pray to that end. This laid the groundwork for the widespread outpouring of the Holy Spirit among Catholics.

The defining event was a retreat in Pittsburgh, Pennsylvania, in February 1967, attended by some twenty Catholic professors and graduate students from Duquesne University. One historian wrote:

> In preparation for the retreat, the participants were asked to read the Book of Acts and David Wilkerson's *The Cross and the Switchblade*. When the group gathered in the chapel on Saturday evening, they experienced a mighty outpouring of the Holy Spirit and some began speaking in tongues.... The fire at Duquesne soon spread to Notre Dame University, the center of American Catholicism. Many of its professors and students received the baptism in the Holy Spirit and spoke in tongues. From there the movement spread rapidly, with Catholic charismatic prayer groups springing up across the country.[12]

What has come to be called the "charismatic movement" swelled to a crescendo in the 1970s, during which time Quin had her Holy Spirit encounter. The ministry of Kathryn Kuhlman introduced thousands of believers to the power of the Holy Spirit in miracles and healings during the 1960s and 1970s. The movement waned somewhat in the 1980s, but is now responsible to a large degree for the rapid growth of Christianity in many nations.

The term "charismatic" is based on the Greek word *charisma*, meaning "a gift of grace," because of the emphasis on the exercise of all the gifts of the Spirit. The term "Pentecostal" derives from a Greek term meaning the fiftieth day after the Passover, when the Jews observed the Feast of Pentecost. It was on this feast day that the Holy Spirit came to the 120 who had been waiting in the Upper Room according to Jesus' instructions (see Acts 1:4; 2:1).

The major distinction between Pentecostal and charismatic doctrine is that the former holds that speaking in tongues is the essential proof (or "initial evidence") that one has been baptized in the Holy Spirit. Charismatic groups, on the other hand, believe that speaking in tongues is an evidence that may or may not follow one's being baptized in the Holy Spirit.

No matter how maligned or misunderstood it may be, the twentieth-century Holy Spirit renewal has definitely changed the face of Christianity around the world.

The Holy Spirit Changes a Family

My own (Ruthanne's) father was a fairly new Christian and a denominational church member when his life was radically changed in the early 1940s. While attending a Pentecostal revival meeting with some coworkers from the bakery where he worked, he received the Holy Spirit and spoke in tongues. Yet when he told my mother about his experience, she was skeptical. "I don't want to know anything about it, and I'm not going to any of those meetings with you," she told him. "Just leave me out of it."

He honored her request, but kept going to the revival meetings as well as to daytime prayer gatherings after work. Soon she became curious about what went on there that caused Dad to have such an interest in spiritual matters. Shortly afterward they both visited a Pentecostal church in our neighborhood, and Mom went forward for prayer to receive the Holy Spirit. Not only was she filled with the Spirit with speaking in tongues; she said she also experienced such waves of laughter that her sides were sore the next day.

A major long-term impact the Holy Spirit made upon my parents' lives was to increase their faith level to allow them to trust God for physical healing. When my older brother was stricken with spinal meningitis, Dad stayed at his bedside through the night, praying for God's healing power to touch him. By the next morning, my brother was well. When I was about eleven years old I was receiving several shots a week for a severe case of eczema, but it was not getting better. One Sunday night my parents asked our pastor to anoint me with oil and pray for my healing. Within a week the eczema was gone, never to return.

At age thirteen I received the Holy Spirit one Sunday night in the prayer room at church after a year of diligent seeking—in those days we often had "tarrying meetings" in the prayer room after evening services. From the time of that experience I always had a great desire to serve the Lord in some type of ministry.

Sometimes I would go with my dad when he preached at a revival meeting conducted by one of his coworkers, or when he led a Bible study at the local county jail. Almost all my activities—teaching children's Sunday school, helping the pastor's wife with child care, and participating in the youth group—revolved around our church. Of course, my Pentecostal upbringing brought with it much rejection by relatives and peers. I also sometimes struggled with my church's prohibition against wearing makeup, and the dress code, which seemed unnecessarily strict. Yet, I knew my experience with the Holy Spirit was real and I never wanted to renounce it.

It's amazing to me to look back over more than fifty years of my life since that night I received the Holy Spirit in the prayer room of a humble little Pentecostal church in Tulsa, Oklahoma.

It was in that same prayer room, at age twenty-two, that I felt the Lord leading me to quit my secretarial job at an evangelistic association and enroll in a Bible school in Missouri. Four years later I met and married John Garlock, a missionary and Bible teacher who joined the Bible school faculty a few months after his wife had died. When I married John—which meant becoming stepmother to two young daughters—I had no idea of the adventures the Holy Spirit had in store for my future.

John also had grown up with a Pentecostal background, but his parents were in full-time ministry. He spent part of his childhood living in northern Ghana, West Africa, when his parents were missionaries there. Then he lived in several different cities of the United States where his father was called to pastor. He shares his own experience of receiving the Holy Spirit.

"Saturated With His Presence"

Having grown up in a minister's home, I understood the "doctrine of the Holy Spirit" long before I had a personal experience to validate it. But my desire to be rational and "scientific" stood in my way. In high school my hobbies were mostly science related, and my friends were the straight-A students. To me, the Pentecostal beliefs about miracles and speaking in tongues seemed rather lowbrow. In fact, I studied the Bible really hard to try and convince myself that my parents were somewhat extreme—that being a good "evangelical" was all I needed in my spiritual life. And I certainly did not want to be involved in ministry as my life's work. I would be a scientist—and not have to deal with the unreliable vagaries of *people*.

But at seventeen I found myself growing hungrier for God, wanting more of his presence and guidance in my life. The more I read the Bible, the more I realized that the answer lay in being filled with the Holy Spirit, which I saw plainly was an experience beyond conversion or being "born again." I began taking every opportunity to pray to receive the Holy Spirit, mostly at the altar of the church where my father was pastor.

In that church was a dear lady named Billie. She was middle-aged, single, very poor and uneducated, but she always stayed to pray at the altar after every meeting. Being aware of my need when I would go to the altar, Billie would get close to me and add her prayers to mine. At first I wished she'd leave me alone. Her clothes always appeared worn out. She looked unkempt and almost homeless—you could tell she didn't bathe very often. Her voice was coarse and loud. However, Billie really knew how to pray, and I knew God was listening. I became so desperate to be closer to him that I was glad to be closer to Billie. One evening, when the Holy Spirit seemed to saturate me with his presence, I broke out speaking in words I could not understand. And I hugged Billie gratefully.

For me the experience changed everything. Science became secondary; serving and pleasing God became the highest priority. I knew he wanted me to go to Bible school, and everything beyond that would be in his hands.

Jesus' Promise Fulfilled

What a huge variety of experiences have come to hungry-hearted people wanting to know God better! From every kind of church, from every kind of background, their desire has gained a divine response. Jesus has sent the Holy Spirit, just as he promised.

Dr. Vinson Synan, a recognized historian of the renewal, writes:

> All of these movements, both Pentecostal and charismatic, have resulted in a major force in Christianity throughout the world with explosive growth rates not seen before in modern times. . . . These "times of refreshing" show that at the end of the Pentecostal century the movement was far from dead and entered the new millennium with undiminished power. Though renewal and revival have always been a part of Christianity, the twentieth century has indeed been the "century of the Holy Spirit."[13]

We close this book by posing the question with which we began: "Who is the Holy Spirit?"

We know he is the Third Person of the Trinity. He is the Comforter and our Advocate. He convicts us of sin; gives hope, joy, and freedom; and seals our inheritance in Christ. He strengthens and encourages, speaks and guides, and empowers us to witness of Jesus' redeeming grace. He brings revelation, gives spiritual gifts, and loves through us with God's love when our human love falls short. He helps us worship, shows us how to pray, prays through us, and enables us to speak in tongues we have not learned.

Jesus promised to send this gift because he knew every believer would need the help of the Holy Spirit to live an overcoming life. Yet the critical question is—*Who is the Holy Spirit to you?* Are you open to receive what has been provided for you by a loving God? The gift is yours for the asking.

Epilogue

As Quin and I were finishing the manuscript for this project, I remembered having met a young couple a few years ago who told me they had received the Holy Spirit through reading our book, *A Woman's Guide to Spirit-Filled Living.* They were students at Christ For The Nations Institute in Dallas at the time, and my husband and I were visiting there while John served as a guest lecturer for a week.

"If only I could find them and get the details of their story!" I told Quin on the phone one day. But I soon forgot about it, since I didn't know their names, which state they came from, or what year they had graduated.

Then we flew to Grand Rapids, Michigan in December 2001 for John to speak at a large church led by a former student who had been in his classes at this same Bible school. It was a busy weekend with John speaking in five services over the two days. On Sunday evening as we were leaving the building, the wife of a staff member called out to me. "We're the couple who received the Holy Spirit after reading your book," she said. "I want to thank you again for writing it—we're leaving soon for the mission field."

I was stunned! Not knowing where to begin, I hadn't even tried to locate them. And now, in the final moments of our visit at this huge church, the Holy Spirit arranged my "divine appointment" with Robin and Clark. When I asked them to share their testimony in this book they happily agreed (their story appears in chapter 3).

This is only one example of how the Holy Spirit intervenes in our lives to help us with things we could never do for ourselves.

Three days after submitting the manuscript for this book, I attended a prayer gathering in New York City near the Ground Zero recovery site where the World Trade Center towers once stood. Such an interesting variety of people came from different backgrounds and different parts of the country—yet the Holy Spirit united us in our purpose to pray for the nation, for the city of New York, and for those who lost loved ones in the tragedy.

One participant, Wendy, performed several sacred dance presentations, which powerfully portrayed the truth of the gospel. *It's obvious that she's had professional training*, I thought as I watched. *I wonder how the Holy Spirit worked in her life to bring her to this place?* So I asked Wendy to share her story.

About sixteen years ago she came to New York to study dance and acting. In 1996 she auditioned for a part in a gospel musical being presented in Brooklyn, and ended up being the dance captain of the chorus. But in all her years in the theater business, she'd never been in a show quite like this one. Before the opening scene, cast members gathered in a circle and held hands to pray. And at the end of each performance they gave an altar call.

For its last week, the show moved to Manhattan to an off-Broadway theater. After the final curtain fell, one of the cast members took Wendy aside. "I believe God is calling you—he wants you to give your life to him," he told her.

"Yes, I want to do that," she replied. After the young man led Wendy in the sinner's prayer, she began attending church regularly. Over the next several months she grew in the Lord and was baptized in water.

"I felt my days in the theater world were numbered—that God was calling me out," Wendy told me. "But I prayed for one more part in a show so I could take care of my financial responsibilities. When I was asked to go on a six-month tour with a dance group I agreed, but it proved to be a big mistake. This was a very worldly group, and I succumbed to the strong temptation to live like they were living. One day one of my friends who wasn't even a Christian said, 'Wendy, this isn't for you.' I went back to New York and asked God to help me live for him. My boyfriend and I both committed our lives to the Lord, then we got married. Our son was born one year later on our anniversary."

From the time she had begun attending church, Wendy occasionally heard people in the congregation speaking in tongues. She wanted the experience, but never pursued it. One day a friend of her husband's came to visit, and as the three sat around the kitchen table, he asked Wendy whether she had received the Holy Spirit.

"No, but I'd like to," she replied.

"He prayed for me, and suddenly my tongue felt like it was getting thicker, and then a new language came out of my mouth as I worshipped the Lord," Wendy said. "After praying like that for a long time, I began weeping. Our friend said, 'Pray over your husband.' When I did, my husband began speaking in tongues very quietly—our prayer languages are quite different from one another. Ever since that day I've been using this gift in worship, prayer, and intercession. Sometimes I sing in tongues and dance during my personal time with the Lord."

After Wendy had left her theater career, the Lord spoke to her one day and said, "I took you out of the world of dance—now I'm sending you back to do it for me." She uses her gift of expression through movement to glorify the Lord, and now has a studio for training others in the craft.

"I feel the Lord instructed me to 'take the devil out of the dance,'" she told me. "This is a gift that God wants us to take back from the world to use for his purposes."

Wendy's story prompted me to say my husband, "The ways of the Holy Spirit are amazing—and yet he keeps amazing me more!" I pray I will never try to put limitations on the Holy Spirit, but that my walk with him will be fresh and new every day. And I pray that you, our readers, will experience—as did Robin, Clark, Wendy, and others in this book—the baptism and renewal of the Holy Spirit.

—*Ruthanne Garlock*

Notes

ONE
Who Is the Holy Spirit?

1. J.I. Packer, *Concise Theology: A Guide to Historic Christian Beliefs* (Wheaton, Ill.: Tyndale House, 1993), computer disk format.
2. James Strong, *The Strongest Strong's Exhaustive Concordance of the Bible* (Grand Rapids, Mich.: Zondervan, 2001), Greek entry #1411.
3. Jack Hayford, "Kingdom Dynamics," in *The Spirit-Filled Life Bible*, Jack Hayford, ed. (Nashville, Tenn.: Thomas Nelson, 1991), 1622.
4. Adapted from Quin Sherrer, *Listen, God Is Speaking to You* (Ann Arbor, Mich.: Servant, 1999), 195.
5. J. Rodman Williams, *The Gift of the Holy Spirit Today* (Plainfield, N.J.: Logos, International, 1980), 29.
6. C.K. Mackintosh, *Genesis to Deuteronomy: Notes on the Pentateuch* (Neptune, N.J.: Loizeaux Brothers, 1972), 58.

TWO
Does the Holy Spirit Make a Difference?

1. John Sherrill, *They Speak with Other Tongues*, (Grand Rapids, Mich.: Chosen/Revell, 1964, 1985), 90.
2. Sherrill, 90.
3. Sherrill, 130.

THREE
How Do I Receive the Holy Spirit?

1. Jack Hayford, *Living the Spirit-Formed Life* (Ventura, Calif.: Regal, 2001), 121.
2. Gordon Lindsay, *Gifts of the Spirit*, vol. 4 (Dallas: Christ for the Nations, 1989), 93.

FOUR
Why Speak in Tongues?

1. Paul Walker, "Holy Spirit Gifts and Power," in *The Spirit-Filled Life Bible*, edited by Jack W. Hayford (Nashville, Tenn.: Thomas Nelson, 1991), 2020.
2. Jack Deere, *Surprised by the Power of the Spirit* (Grand Rapids, Mich.: Zondervan, 1993), 139.
3. Judson Cornwall, *Praying the Scriptures* (Lake Mary, Fla.: Creation House, 1990), 212-13.
4. George Stormont, *Smith Wigglesworth: A Man Who Walked With God* (Tulsa, Okla.: Harrison House, 1989), 138-39.
5. Corrie ten Boom, *Marching Orders for the End Battle* (Fort Washington, Penn.: Christian Literature Crusade, 1969), 33-34.
6. H.B. Garlock, *Before We Kill and Eat You*, Ruthanne Garlock, ed., (Dallas: Christ for the Nations, 1974), 100 [now out of print].

FIVE
Are Hang-Ups Holding You Back?

1. Adapted from Quin Sherrer and Ruthanne Garlock, *A Woman's Guide to Spirit-Filled Living* (Ann Arbor, Mich.: Servant, 1996), 150-52.
2. Arthur Wallis, *Pray in the Spirit* (Fort Washington, Penn.: Christian Literature Crusade, 1970), 82-83, 86.
3. Lindsay, 65.
4. Catherine Marshall, *The Helper* (Grand Rapids, Mich.: Baker, 1978), 66-67.

SIX
How Can I Walk in the Spirit?

1. W.E. Vine, *Vine's Expository Dictionary of Old and New Testament Words*, vol. 3 (Old Tappan, N.J.: Revell, 1981), 195.
2. David Wilkerson, "What It Means to Walk in the Spirit," *Times Square Church Pulpit Series*, August 15, 1994, 1.
3. A.B. Simpson, "Walking in the Spirit," *Herald of His Coming*, February 1995, 5. Reprinted from A.B. Simpson, *The Gentle Love of the Holy Spirit* (Camp Hill, Penn.: Christian Publications, 1983).
4. Adapted from Sherrer, 136-37.
5. Elizabeth Alves, *The Mighty Warrior* (Bulverde, Tex.: Intercessors International, 1992), 69-70.

SEVEN
Renewal That Endures

1. Ted Haggard, "A Pastor's Prayer Principles," *Ministries Today*, November-December 1994, 17.

EIGHT
The Holy Spirit in History

1. Donald Lee Barnett and Jeffrey P. McGregor, *Speaking in Other Tongues: A Scholarly Defense* (Seattle: Community Chapel, 1986), 229.
2. Daniel G. Reid, ed., *Dictionary of Christianity in America* (Downers Grove, Ill.: InterVarsity, 1990), 1241.
3. Barnett and McGregor, 242.
4. Quoted from Guy Chevreau, *Catch the Fire* (Toronto: Harper Collins, 1995), 82-83.
5. Barnett and McGregor, 252.
6. Barnett and McGregor, 253.
7. Barnett and McGregor, 254.
8. Stanley Howard Frodsham, *With Signs Following*, rev. ed. (Springfield, Mo.: Gospel Publishing House, 1946), 20.
9. William Booth-Clibborn, *The Baptism in the Holy Spirit*, 4th ed. (Dallas: Voice of Healing Publishing, 1962), 43.
10. Booth-Clibborn, 71-72.
11. Stanley M. Burgess and Gary B. McGee, eds., *Dictionary of Pentecostal and Charismatic Movements* (Grand Rapids, Mich.: Zondervan, 1988), 132.
12. Eddie L. Hyatt, *2,000 Years of Charismatic Christianity* (Dallas: Hyatt International Ministries, 1998), 197-98.
13. Vinson Synan, *The Century of the Holy Spirit* (Nashville, Tenn.: Thomas Nelson, 2001), 12.

Recommended Reading

Ahn, Ché. *Hosting the Holy Spirit*. Ventura, Calif.: Renew Books, 2000.

Barnett, Donald Lee, and Jeffrey P. McGregor. *Speaking in Other Tongues: A Scholarly Defense*. Seattle: Community Chapel Publications, 1986.

Bennett, Dennis, and Rita Bennett. *The Holy Spirit and You*. Gainsville, Fla.: Bridge-Logos, 2000.

Burgess, Stanley M., and Gary B. McGee, eds. *Dictionary of Pentecostal and Charismatic Movements*. Grand Rapids, Mich.: Zondervan, 1988.

Cymbala, Jim. *Fresh Power*. Grand Rapids, Mich.: Zondervan, 2001.

Deere, Jack. *Surprised by the Power of the Spirit*. Grand Rapids, Mich.: Zondervan, 1993.

Hayford, Jack. *Living the Spirit-Formed Life*. Ventura, Calif.: Regal, 2001.

Hayford, Jack, ed. *The Spirit-Filled Life Bible*. Nashville, Tenn.: Thomas Nelson, 1991, revised 2002.

Horton, Stanley M. *What the Bible Says About the Holy Spirit*. Springfield, Mo.: Gospel Publishing House, 1997.

Hyatt, Eddie L. *2,000 Years of Charismatic Christianity*. Dallas: Hyatt International Ministries, 1998.

Lindsay, Gordon. *Gifts of the Spirit*. 4 vols. Dallas: Christ for the Nations, 1989.

Marshall, Catherine. *Something More*. Carmel, N.Y.: Guideposts Books, 1974.

————. *The Helper.* Grand Rapids, Mich.: Baker, 1978.

Sheets, Dutch. *The Beginner's Guide to Intercession.* Ann Arbor, Mich.: Servant, 2001.

————. **Intercessory Prayer.** Ventura, Calif.: Regal, 1996.

Sherrer, Quin. *Listen, God Is Speaking to You.* Ann Arbor, Mich.: Servant, 1999.

Sherrer, Quin, and Ruthanne Garlock. *A Woman's Guide to Spiritual Warfare.* Ann Arbor, Mich.: Servant, 1991.

————. *The Spiritual Warrior's Prayer Guide.* Ann Arbor, Mich.: Servant, 1992.

————. *A Woman's Guide to Spirit-Filled Living.* Ann Arbor, Mich.: Servant, 1996.

————. *How to Pray for Your Children.* Ventura, Calif.: Regal, 1998.

————. *Prayers Women Pray.* Ann Arbor, Mich.: Servant, 1998.

————. *Praying Prodigals Home.* Ventura, Calif.: Regal, 2000.

————. *Prayer Partnerships.* Ann Arbor, Mich.: Servant, 2001.

Sherrill, John. *They Speak with Other Tongues.* Grand Rapids, Mich.: Chosen/Revell, 1964, 1985.

Storms, Sam. *A Beginner's Guide to Spiritual Gifts.* Ann Arbor, Mich.: Servant, 2002.

Sumrall, Lester. *The Gifts and Ministries of the Holy Spirit.* New Kensington, Penn.: Whitaker House, 1993.

Synan, Vinson. *The Century of the Holy Spirit.* Nashville, Tenn.: Thomas Nelson, 2001.

Torrey, R.A. *The Person and Work of the Holy Spirit.* New Kensington, Penn.: Whitaker House, 1996.

Wagner, C. Peter. *The Acts of the Holy Spirit.* Ventura, Calif.: Regal, 1994.

Wallis, Arthur. *Pray in the Spirit.* Fort Washington, Penn.: Christian Literature Crusade, 1970.

Warner, Wayne. *Smith Wigglesworth: The Anointing of His Spirit.* Ann Arbor, Mich.: Servant, 1994.

White, John. *When the Spirit Comes With Power.* Downers Grove, Ill.: InterVarsity, 1988.

Other Books in
The Beginner's Guide Series
Include: